"Channeling the likes of Owen, Bunyan, M'Cheyne, and Calvin, Brian Hedges cares for the Christian's soul with the expertise of a seasoned pastor and a wise shepherd. He instructs the reader in the needful and often-neglected spiritual discipline of watchfulness. If you would enjoy Christ more, safeguard your soul with greater effectiveness, and live the faith-filled life more intentionally, devour these pages. It will do your soul good and sow seeds for a life of devotion to Christ."

—Jason Helopoulos, Associate Pastor, University Reformed Church, Lansing, Michigan, and Author of *A Neglected Grace: Family Worship in the Christian Home*

"Many Christians today are unaware of one of the most fundamental spiritual disciplines necessary to advance in the Christian life—namely, watchfulness. By drawing from the vast riches of Scripture and the writings of Puritan divines, Brian Hedges shines a much-needed light on this often-neglected subject. This book will elevate your pursuit of personal holiness as it brings to the forefront of your mind the eternal benefits of watching over your heart and being alert for your enemy."

—Steven J. Lawson, President, OnePassion Ministries, Dallas, Texas

"Doctrine is easier to learn than godliness. Yet true doctrine is according to godliness. Brian Hedges faithfully guides his readers to cultivate godliness through watchfulness by answering the questions what, why, how, when, and who. Drawing particularly from the insights of Owen, Bunyan, and M'Cheyne, he makes the dead speak to us with a fresh voice on a neglected topic for the refreshment of our souls."

—Ryan M. McGraw, Morton H. Smith Professor of Systematic Theology, Greenville Presbyterian Theological Seminary

"We need constant reminders to be watchful lest we fall. And when these reminders come clothed in grace and pastoral sensitivity, they are all the more welcome. Brian Hedges has put together a small gem of a book that urges us to greater care and watchfulness, with gospel-driven exhortation and warnings to busy Christians. Timely and necessary."

—Derek W. H. Thomas, Senior Minister, First Presbyterian Church, Columbia, South Carolina; Chancellor's Professor, Reformed Theological Seminary; and Teaching Fellow, Ligonier Ministries

Watchfulness

Watchfulness

RECOVERING A LOST SPIRITUAL DISCIPLINE

Brian G. Hedges

Reformation Heritage Books
Grand Rapids, Michigan

Reformation Heritage Books
2965 Leonard St. NE
Grand Rapids, MI 49525
616-977-0889
orders@heritagebooks.org
www.heritagebooks.org

Printed in the United States of America
18 19 20 21 22 23/10 9 8 7 6 5 4 3 2 1

Library of Congress Cataloging-in-Publication Data

Names: Hedges, Brian G., author.
Title: Watchfulness : recovering a lost spiritual discipline / Brian G Hedges.
Description: Grand Rapids, Michigan : Reformation Heritage Books, 2018.
Identifiers: LCCN 2017061085 (print) | LCCN 2018001618 (ebook) | ISBN
     9781601785954 (epub) | ISBN 9781601785947 (pbk. : alk. paper)
Subjects: LCSH: Spiritual life—Christianity. | Vigilance (Psychology) |
     Attention—Religious aspects—Christianity.
Classification: LCC BV4509.5 (ebook) | LCC BV4509.5 .H44 2018 (print) |
     DDC 248.4/6–dc23
LC record available at https://lccn.loc.gov/2017061085

For additional Reformed literature, request a free book list from Reformation Heritage Books at the above regular or e-mail address.

To Dad

I want a principle within
Of watchful, godly fear,
A sensibility of sin,
A pain to feel it near.
I want the first approach to feel
Of pride or wrong desire,
To catch the wandering of my will,
And quench the kindling fire.

From thee that I no more may stray,
No more thy goodness grieve,
Grant me the filial awe, I pray,
The tender conscience give.
Quick as the apple of an eye,
O God, my conscience make;
Awake my soul when sin is nigh,
And keep it still awake.

Almighty God of truth and love,
To me thy power impart;
The mountain from my soul remove,
The hardness from my heart.
O may the least omission pain
My reawakened soul,
And drive me to that blood again,
Which makes the wounded whole.

—CHARLES WESLEY, 1749

Contents

Foreword

Every once in awhile I read a book and think, "I wish I had written this book." This is one of those books. The funny thing is, I *could* have written it. But it's a good thing I didn't because it wouldn't have been nearly as thorough or helpful as Brian Hedges's book.

Here's what I mean. Back in 1991, as I was finishing the original edition of *Spiritual Disciplines for the Christian Life*, J. I. Packer graciously agreed to write the foreword. After he had done so, he encouraged me to consider including a chapter on "watching." (Okay, so I might have written a *chapter* on watchfulness, not an entire book.)

It was too close to publication to add that much material, but it wouldn't have mattered if I'd been given the time. I wasn't even sure what Packer was referring to by "watching." As an expert on the Puritans, he was, of course, encouraging me to write about a subject often addressed by authors from the beginning of the Puritan period, such as Richard Rogers, all the way through to those at the end of the era, such as John Bunyan.

Dr. Packer assumed, since I quoted so frequently from the Puritans in my *Spiritual Disciplines* manuscript—especially

John Owen, John Flavel, John Bunyan, and Jonathan Edwards, not to mention later writers with the Puritan spirit, such as Robert Murray M'Cheyne and Charles Spurgeon—that I was familiar with their respective writings on "watching." The fact of the matter was that I had read few of those particular works. I certainly hadn't given sufficient thought to the biblical texts on watchfulness in a way that prepared me to write a biblical theology on the theme and apply it to the lives of my readers.

Reading this book has made me thankful that Brian Hedges has done both. In the volume you are holding, he has brought together the biblical teaching on watching over our souls and seasoned it with insights from great works by godly men who were both passionate and practical about watchfulness.

This book is needed. It fills a space on the subject of the Christian life that has been empty far too long.

—Donald S. Whitney
Professor of Biblical Spirituality
The Southern Baptist Seminary,
Louisville, Kentucky

Acknowledgments

I want to thank the folks at Reformation Heritage Books for their partnership in publishing this book. Thanks to Joel Beeke for his interest in this project, to Jay Collier for enthusiastically supporting and shepherding the book from proposal to publication, and to Annette Gysen for her proficiency and efficiency as an editor. Thanks also to Steve Renkema, my initial contact with RHB, for first expressing interest in this book.

I am grateful to the elders and members of Fulkerson Park Baptist Church for continuing to provide generous time off for writing.

To Holly and the kids: you are God's best earthly blessings in my life. Thank you for cheerfully supporting my calling to serve others through both the spoken and written word.

Thanks to Don Whitney not only for writing the foreword but for charting a course for studying Puritan literature on the spiritual disciplines in his excellent book *Spiritual Disciplines for the Christian Life*.

Finally, I have dedicated this book to my father, Ronnie Hedges. His prayerful, Christ-centered watchfulness continues to bear the fruit of humble integrity, winsome holiness, gentle wisdom, and patient love. Thank you, Dad, for watching your life and doctrine and for always pointing me and others to Christ.

Introduction
The Lost Spiritual Discipline

In recent decades the evangelical church has seen a resurging interest in the practical aspects of Christian spirituality. Books on spiritual transformation and the spiritual disciplines line our shelves. Many of these are helpful, offering wise instruction on practices such as meditation, prayer, and fasting.[1] But one discipline rarely appears in these catalogs of devotional habits: watchfulness.

Yet watchfulness is as necessary to a healthy spiritual life as meditation and prayer. Jesus tells His disciples to "watch and pray, lest you enter into temptation" (Matt. 26:41). The letters of Paul, Peter, and John sound the same note, urging us to exercise moral vigilance and watchful prayer (1 Cor. 16:13; Gal. 6:1; Col. 4:2; 1 Tim. 4:16; 1 Peter 4:7; 2 John 8). And Hebrews commands mutual watchfulness and exhortation

---

1. Some of my favorites are Donald S. Whitney, *Spiritual Disciplines for the Christian Life*, rev. ed. (Colorado Springs: NavPress, 2014); John Piper, *When I Don't Desire God: How to Fight for Joy* (Wheaton, Ill.: Crossway, 2004); Timothy Keller, *Prayer: Experiencing Awe and Intimacy with God* (New York: Dutton, 2014); and David Mathis, *Habits of Grace: Enjoying Jesus through the Spiritual Disciplines* (Wheaton, Ill.: Crossway, 2016). On spiritual transformation, see my book *Christ Formed in You: The Power of the Gospel for Personal Change* (Wapwallopen, Pa.: Shepherd Press, 2010).

while also reminding us to obey those leaders who keep watch over our souls (Heb. 3:12; 13:17).

Watchfulness for All Seasons

All believers, regardless of their station and season in life, need to be watchful. Consider Beth, a married woman in her thirties with three children, six years old and under. She loves Jesus and thrived in her walk with Christ during her college and single years. But the domestic, often mundane challenges of motherhood are more difficult than Beth expected. She feels distant from God. She longs for the days when she could quietly spend hours over her Bible and journal. The chaos of corralling her children from one activity to another makes it hard for her to focus on spiritual things. Beth needs to become more attentive to her state of heart and learn how to stay connected to Jesus throughout the day.

Nathan, on the other hand, is a college-aged believer struggling with pornography. He feels terrible when he fails and quickly repents. While he tries to read the Bible and pray every day, he is missing something in his spiritual regimen. His use of time lacks intentionality. His quiet times are disconnected from his other habits in solitude. Despite regular sin struggles, he underestimates the danger of temptation. Like the disciples in the garden, Nathan needs to learn how to watch and pray against temptation's subtle power.

Craig is a spiritually mature Christian man entering midlife. He has been married for twenty-five years and has four children in middle school and high school. He is a veteran lay leader in his church and enjoys a close walk with God. But Craig is saddled with many burdens, and his emotional resilience isn't what it used to be. He faces new temptations in his fifties and needs Jesus more than ever. Paul's words, "Let him who thinks he stands take heed lest he fall," echo in his mind. Craig is searching for practical ways to put this into practice.[2]

While their seasons of life are quite different, Beth, Nathan, and Craig have a common need: the consistent exercise of vigilance over their hearts and active dependence on the Lord's sustaining grace. As varied as their temptations are, Paul's exhortation applies: "Watch, stand fast in the faith, be brave, be strong" (1 Cor. 16:13).

The Puritans on Watchfulness

Past believers understood the need for watchfulness and spoke of it often. This was especially true of the sixteenth- and seventeenth-century English Puritans and their evangelical heirs in the following centuries. In their sermons, letters, diaries, and manuals on spirituality, these saints commended the practice of watching along with better-known disciplines like meditation and prayer.

Richard Rogers, for example, was an early Puritan who published a substantial book called *Seven Treatises* in 1602.[3] Divided into seven parts, the nine-hundred-page compendium

---

2. While these are fictional examples, they reflect the challenges and temptations common to hundreds of believers in similar life situations.

3. The fuller title is *SEVEN TREATISES, CONTAINING SUCH DIRECTION AS IS GATHERED OUT OF THE HOLY SCRIPTURES, leading and guiding to true happiness, both in this life, and in the life to come: and may be called the practice of Christianity.* One scholarly source calls Rogers "the most influential of the spiritual authors," noting that *Seven Treatises* "went through six editions between 1603 and 1630, with a further five editions of an abridgment by Stephen Egerton.... The influence of Seven treatises can be traced in the lives of a whole generation of Puritan laymen." Patrick Collinson, Arnold Hunt, and Alexandra Walsam, "Religious Publishing in England 1557–1640," in *The Cambridge History of the Book in Britain*, vol. 4, *1557–1695*, ed. John

on Christian living explores the full spectrum of religious life and experience, from questions of conversion and assurance to the public and private means of pursuing godliness, and from daily directions for walking with God to the various hindrances and privileges of the true Christian—and more.[4] In the third treatise, Rogers discusses "the means whereby a godly life is helped and continued" and divides these helps into two categories: public and private. The private means include things you might expect, like meditation, prayer, and fasting. But first on Rogers's list of private helps is watchfulness, "which is worthily set in the first place, seeing it is as an eye to all the rest, to see them well and rightly used."[5]

The implication is clear: neglect watchfulness and you will hinder other spiritual practices. Watchfulness is the whetstone of the spiritual disciplines, the one practice that keeps the other habits sharp.

In their teaching on watchfulness, the Puritans commonly quoted Proverbs 4:23 (KJV): "Keep thy heart with all diligence; for out of it are the issues of life." John Flavel wrote an entire book on this verse, *A Saint Indeed (or, The Great Work*

Barnard, D. F. McKenzie, and Maureen Bell (Cambridge: Cambridge University Press, 2002), 42. Subsequent citations from *Seven Treatises* (London, 1616).

4. In the second of three addresses to Christian readers in the *Seven Treatises*, fellow Puritan Ezekiel Culverwell says, "In my simple opinion it might in one principal respect be called the Anatomy of the soul, wherein not only the great and principal parts are laid open, but every vein and little nerve are so discovered, that we may as it were, with the eye behold, as the right constitution of the whole and every part of a true Christian; so the manifold defects and imperfections thereof." Rogers, *Seven Treatises*, A4v–A5r.

5. Rogers, *Seven Treatises*, 243. See also Richard Rogers, *Holy Helps for a Godly Life* (Grand Rapids: Reformation Heritage Books, 2018), 41. This is a modernized edition of Rogers's third treatise. Unless otherwise noted, all subsequent quotations are from this edition.

of a Christian Opened and Pressed).[6] "The greatest difficulty in conversion is to win the heart to God and the greatest difficulty after conversion is to keep the heart with God," writes Flavel on the opening page.[7] What follows is a tour de force in Christian spirituality, a traveler's guide that maps and marks twelve seasons of Christian experience through which the heart must be watched and kept.

Some of the most helpful companions in my journey have been John Owen (1616–1683), John Bunyan (1628–1688), and Robert Murray M'Cheyne (1813–1843). Owen was a non-conformist pastor and theologian during the Puritan era. For nearly two decades his books on mortification, temptation, indwelling sin, apostasy, spiritual-mindedness, communion with God, the glory of Christ, the evidences of faith, and the work of the Holy Spirit have been the richest portion of my devotional diet. Several years ago I noticed that Owen frequently includes watching alongside meditation and prayer in describing the means for mortifying sin, nourishing spiritual affections, and cultivating communion with God. For example, in his treatise *The Grace and Duty of Being Spiritually Minded*, Owen says, "It is no ordinary nor easy thing to preserve our affections pure, entire, and steady, in their vigorous adherence unto spiritual things.... Watchfulness, prayer, faith in exercise, and a daily examination of ourselves, are required hereunto. For want of a due attendance unto these things, and

---

6. This book has now been modernized and republished as *A Treatise on Keeping the Heart* and is widely available in various formats online. My quotations will be from volume 5 in *The Works of John Flavel* (1820; repr., Edinburgh: Banner of Truth Trust, 1968).

7. John Flavel, *Saint Indeed*, in *Works*, 5:423.

that, with respect unto this end…many, even before they are aware, die away as to all power and vigour of spiritual life."[8]

Owen mentions watching dozens of times in his works, and his well-known treatise *Of Temptation* provides the most helpful study of watchfulness I have found.[9] Owen was an adept soul-physician, an expert in the pathology of sin, who diagnosed the subtleties of temptation and skillfully prescribed the biblical cure to "watch and pray." We'll return to Owen often in this book, mining this treasure trove of rich, practical, gospel wisdom for all it's worth.

Watching on the Journey and in the Battle
My second companion has been John Bunyan, whose allegories *The Pilgrim's Progress* and *The Holy War* have furnished thousands of believers with powerful, memorable illustrations of Christian doctrine and experience. *The Pilgrim's Progress* vividly depicts the Christian life as a journey. Bunyan's story of Christian's odyssey to the Celestial City first captured my imagination when I was a child. It is a picture gallery of the "molestations, troubles, wars, captivities, cries, groans, frights, and fears"[10] common to spiritual experience. In its pages Bunyan illustrates the practical need for watchfulness against the numerous dangers that beset us on the way to heaven: discouragement (the Slough of Despond), temptation (the Valley

8. John Owen, *The Grace and Duty of Being Spiritually Minded*, in *The Works of John Owen*, ed. William Goold (1862; repr., Edinburgh: Banner of Truth Trust, 1966), 7:486.

9. John Owen, *Of Temptation: The Nature and Power Of It; The Danger of Entering Into It; and The Means of Preventing that Danger*, in *Works*, 6:87–151.

10. As Mr. Sagacity describes Christian's journey to Christiana in part 2. John Bunyan, *The Pilgrim's Progress* (1895; repr., Edinburgh: Banner of Truth Trust, 1977), 203.

of Humiliation), worldliness (Vanity Fair), despair (Giant Despair and Doubting Castle), and sloth (the Enchanted Ground). *The Holy War* portrays the spiritual battle waged by King Shaddai and his son Emmanuel against Diabolus and his horde for the city of Mansoul. In this allegory Bunyan teaches the believer's need to guard and fortify his or her soul once it has been reclaimed by grace.

Bunyan knew his Bible well and plundered its imagery in these books, pressing upon his readers both the warnings and promises of Scripture. I have used Bunyan's allegories generously in this book, hoping not only to explain but also to illustrate the nature, need, and practice of watchfulness.

"Make Me as Holy as a Pardoned Sinner Can Be Made"

My third companion in learning about watchfulness is Robert Murray M'Cheyne, a nineteenth-century Scottish pastor who died when he was only twenty-nine years old. A singular anointing marked his ministry. He often prayed, "Lord, make me as holy as a pardoned sinner can be made."[11] The *Memoir & Remains of Robert Murray M'Cheyne*, edited by M'Cheyne's friend Andrew Bonar, is a spiritual classic that continues to stir the hearts of believers today.

An excerpt from M'Cheyne's diary puts hands and feet on the actual practice of watchfulness. In the final year of his life, M'Cheyne wrote an insightful examination of his heart and life, which he labeled "Personal Reformation." M'Cheyne mentioned watching three times in these pages, including this

---

11. *Memoir & Remains of Robert Murray M'Cheyne*, ed. Andrew A. Bonar (1892; repr., Edinburgh: Banner of Truth Trust, 1966), 159.

statement: "If I would be filled with the Spirit, I feel I must read the Bible more, pray more, and watch more."[12]

M'Cheyne's diary is yet another indication that past believers considered watchfulness a staple component of their spiritual lives. As we'll see in chapter 3, M'Cheyne's spiritual regimen shows what the earnest, Christ-centered, grace-driven practice of self-examination and watchfulness looks like in daily life.

If you share M'Cheyne's passion for holiness, watchfulness will be crucial to your growth in sanctification. If you do not burn for holiness, you are already off your watch.

A Road Map for Watchfulness

I've organized this book around a journalist's five investigative questions—what, why, how, when, and who[13]—and these questions correspond to the book's five chapters.

Think of these questions as key locations on a road map for watchfulness. With each leg of the journey, I have aimed to answer each question with a combination of meditation, illustration, application, and relevant quotations from the best historic literature on the subject. My primary conversation partners have been Owen, Bunyan, and M'Cheyne, but I've also quoted other Puritan authors and have included numerous sidebars that feature additional insights, directions, and examples, drawn mostly from Puritan authors.[14] Each chapter

---

12. Bonar, *Memoir & Remains*, 154. See appendix 1 for the complete "Personal Reformation."

13. Sometimes "where" is also included in this list. I'm conflating "when" and "where" into one category.

14. In many of these quotations, I have updated the spelling and punctuation.

concludes with a series of "Examine and Apply" questions designed to foster reflection, self-examination, and personal application. My hope is that these chapters will chart a course toward greater watchfulness, increased holiness, and deeper communion with our triune God.

One reason I have written this book is because I need to read it. The older I become, the more I see the threats and hazards in Christian experience. Not everyone who starts well finishes well. Many aspire, but few attain. The dangers of backsliding and the warnings against apostasy are real. The deeper I understand myself and my Savior, the more I realize how weak I am, how patient He is, and how utterly dependent upon Him I am for everything.

These words from Robert Robinson's old hymn reverberate often in the echo chamber of my soul. They serve as a fitting coda to this introduction. They remind us why watchfulness is needed (because our hearts are prone to wander) and point us to the only power that can keep us (God's goodness and grace, which binds and seals our hearts for glory):

> Oh, to grace how great a debtor
> Daily I'm constrained to be!
> Let Thy goodness, like a fetter,
> Bind my wandering heart to Thee:
> Prone to wander, Lord, I feel it,
> Prone to leave the God I love;
> Here's my heart, oh, take and seal it;
> Seal it for Thy courts above.[15]

---

15. Robert Robinson, "Come, Thou Fount of Every Blessing" (1758), in the public domain.

Chapter 1

What?

The Nature of Watchfulness

[Watchfulness is]...a universal carefulness and diligence, exercising itself in and by all ways and means
prescribed by God, over our hearts and ways, the baits
and methods of Satan, the occasions and advantages of
sin in the world, that we be not entangled.

—John Owen, *Of Temptation: The Nature and Power
of It; the Danger of Entering Into It; and
the Means of Preventing that Danger*

The Christian life is a journey, a race, and a battle. As pilgrims, we travel the long winding road from the City of
Destruction to the Celestial City. As athletes, we are called to
forget what lies behind and, with eyes fixed on Jesus, to cast
aside every hindrance to completing the race of faith. And as
soldiers, we must ready ourselves for battle by putting on the
gospel armor and relying on the wisdom and strength of Jesus,
our brother, captain, and king.

These biblical metaphors have shaped the Christian
imagination for centuries.[1] Implicit in each picture is the need

---

1. For example, in his sermon "The Christian's Watch," Richard Sibbes
employs each of these metaphors in his list of reasons why "the carriage of a
Christian in this world is an estate of watching until Christ come home." In

for eyes-wide-open watchfulness. In the ancient world, travel was fraught with danger. Believers are citizens of heaven but pilgrims on earth, strangers in a strange land beset by dangers, toils, and snares. The race set before us is not a one-hundred-yard dash, but a marathon strewn with obstacles. And soldiers at war have enemies. Vigilance is not optional. We must be on our watch.

But what is watchfulness? We will begin this chapter by analyzing John Owen's definition of watchfulness. Then we will dig into the biblical terminology and tease out four ingredients of this needed, but often neglected, spiritual discipline.

Defining Watchfulness

What is watchfulness? Here is John Owen's definition, given in his treatise *Of Temptation*:

> A universal carefulness and diligence, exercising itself in and by all ways and means prescribed by God, over our hearts and ways, the baits and methods of Satan, the occasions and advantages of sin in the world, that we be not entangled.[2]

This definition will reward closer investigation. You may feel like you've got it, but you don't. As Holmes tells Watson, "You see, but you do not observe."[3] So slow down. Put on your

---

The Works of Richard Sibbes, ed. Alexander B. Grosart (1862; repr., Edinburgh: Banner of Truth Trust, 2001), 7:300. For more on these metaphors, see my book *Active Spirituality: Grace and Effort in the Christian Life* (Wapwallopen, Pa.: Shepherd Press, 2014).

2. Owen, *Of Temptation*, in *Works*, 6:100–101.

3. Arthur Conan Doyle, "A Scandal in Bohemia," in *Great Cases of Sherlock Holmes* (Franklin, Pa.: The Franklin Library, 1987), 6.

deerstalker hat, dust off your magnifying glass, and settle in for some detective work as we examine this dense Puritan prose.

"*Carefulness*": To be watchful is to be careful. Carefulness suggests attentiveness and alertness, caution and concern. To watch is to care about, to pay attention to, and to take heed to certain aspects of our lives. The antonym of carefulness is care*less*ness. Watchfulness is the opposite of a laissez-faire approach to one's inner life. If you never search your soul, examine your behavior, or take account of your thoughts, words, motives, and actions, then you are not watchful.

"*Diligence*": To watch is not only to be careful but also to be *persistently* careful. Diligence is persistence. If you only examine yourself the way you do laundry (on, say, Wednesdays and Fridays), then you're not watchful. Watchfulness is not haphazard. The watchful believer never takes a day off.

"*Universal carefulness and diligence*": This means complete, comprehensive carefulness. Watchfulness is not selective. If you are cautious and measured in church conversations but careless with words the rest of the week, you are not watchful. Universal watchfulness means taking *all* commands and prohibitions seriously—and doing so in all circumstances and situations.

"*Exercising itself*": Watchfulness is not passive, but active. It involves effort, exertion, action, and holy sweat. Watchfulness is the spiritual equivalent to mixed martial arts or ultimate fighting.

"*Exercising itself in and by all ways and means prescribed by God*": Watchfulness recognizes and submits to the instruction of God's word. God has prescribed *ways* and *means*. He has laid out ways for living: ways of love, humility, justice, holiness, mercy, and peace. And He has given means for living in these ways, what theologians often call the means of grace: meditation, prayer, worship, and more. We'll talk more about these means and their relationship to watchfulness in chapter 3. For now, note that watchfulness involves a rightful use of all the means God prescribes. Again, there is no cafeteria-styled obedience here.

"Over our hearts and ways": The preposition "over" is followed by three phrases. These phrases show what we are to be careful about. We watch "over our hearts and ways." This involves self-awareness and self-examination. As Paul tells Timothy, we need to watch both our life and doctrine (1 Tim. 4:16).

"Over…the baits and methods of Satan": We are also to watch over the enemy of our souls, with all his strategies and devices. Remember Peter's warning? "Be sober, be [watchful];[4] because your adversary the devil walks about like a roaring lion, seeking whom he may devour" (1 Peter 5:8). To watch, then, means to "watch out"! To beware. Your enemy is more unrelenting than a Black Rider hunting the Ring of Power. He is more vicious than an angry cobra cornered by a mongoose. He never goes on vacation. Watch your enemy because he is watching you.

"Over…the occasions and advantages of sin": This means watching out for the circumstances and situations that give sin a foothold in our lives. Jesus says, "Watch and pray, lest you enter into temptation" (Mark 14:38). Paul writes, "Make no provision for the flesh, to fulfill its lusts" (Rom. 13:14).

"In the world": The world here is not planet Earth. It's the fallen world system that lives in rebellion to God. The world is Satan's ally. He is the "ruler of this world" and the "god of

---

4. Or vigilant. "Watchful" is the marginal reading in the NKJV.

this age" (John 12:31; 2 Cor. 4:4). John says, "The whole world lies under the sway of the wicked one" (1 John 5:19). Isaac Watts asks, "Is this vile world a friend to grace to help me on to God?"[5] The clear answer is no. The apostle James makes this clear: "Adulterers and adulteresses! Do you not know that friendship with the world is enmity with God? Whoever therefore wants to be a friend of the world makes himself an enemy of God" (James 4:4).

"That we be not entangled": This final phrase is the purpose clause. The reason we should be watchful is so that we will not be entangled. To be entangled is to be encumbered, ensnared, tripped up. Entanglement is the opposite of freedom. On the surface, watchfulness may sound cumbersome, but this is a lie. Richard Rogers notes that "watchfulness is counted too strict until people be well acquainted with it." But "if you are a stranger to watchfulness, look to fall often, I mean to fall dangerously.... Look to find many wounds in your soul and to lack many comforts in your life."[6]

To cultivate watchfulness is to preserve freedom—from the world and its snares; from sin and its enslaving power; and from the temptations, deceptions, and accusations of our adversary the devil.

Watchfulness in the Bible

The New Testament uses a fistful of words that could be translated "watch" in English. All these words are important, and a quick survey of their meanings and usage will help us understand the nature of watchfulness.

---

5. Isaac Watts, "Am I a Soldier of the Cross?" (1721), in the public domain.
6. Rogers, *Holy Helps*, 43–44, 47.

First, consider the word *blepō*, which means "to see."[7]
While this word denotes the physical act of seeing, sometimes
it carries moral and spiritual connotations. For example, in
2 John 8, it is used to exhort believers to carefully observe
their own lives. We see the same use in Ephesians 5:15: "See
then that you walk [carefully],[8] not as fools but as wise." And
1 Corinthians 10:12 says: "Therefore let him who thinks he
stands *take heed* lest he fall." This is the word Jesus uses in
the parable of the soils, when He tells His disciples to "take
heed" to what they hear (Mark 4:24).[9] At other times this
word means to be on guard or to beware of danger (cf. Mark
12:38; 13:33). Paul uses this word to alert his readers about
false teachers (Phil. 3:2) and the dangers of carnal, conten-
tious behavior in the church (Gal. 5:15). We also see this word
in Hebrews 3:12, a passage we will return to later: "*Beware*,
brethren, lest there be in any of you an evil heart of unbelief
in departing from the living God."

The second word, *grēgoreō*, means "to be on the alert" or
"to be awake."[10] This is the word used for Jesus's warning to
His disciples in the garden: "*Watch* and pray, lest you enter into
temptation. The spirit indeed is willing, but the flesh is weak"
(Matt. 26:41).[11] But this word also suggests moral alertness and
spiritual vigilance. Paul uses this word in 1 Corinthians 16:13:

---

7. This word is used 132 times in the New Testament and is usually translated as "see" or "look."

8. Or circumspectly. "Carefully" is the marginal reading in the NKJV.

9. Cf. Luke 8:18, where He says, "Take heed *how* you hear," where the
adverb *pōs* indicates the manner of hearing rather than the content of the mes-
sage heard.

10. *Grēgoreō* is used twenty-two times in the New Testament.

11. Cf. also vv. 38, 40; Mark 14:34, 37, 38.

"*Watch*, stand fast in the faith, be brave, be strong" and in Colossians 4:2: "Continue earnestly in prayer, being *vigilant* in it with thanksgiving." And this is the term Peter uses in 1 Peter 5:8: "Be sober, be [*watchful*]; because your adversary the devil walks about like a roaring lion, seeking whom he may devour."

The third word translated "watch," *prosechō*, means "to be in a state of alert" or "to pay close attention to something."[12] In Luke 21:34 Jesus says, "But *take heed* to yourselves, lest your hearts be weighed down with carousing, drunkenness, and cares of this life, and that Day come on you unexpectedly." We also find it in Hebrews 2:1: "Therefore we must *give the more earnest heed* to the things we have heard, lest we drift away" and in Paul's charge to the Ephesian elders in Acts 20:28: "Therefore *take heed* to yourselves and to all the flock, among which the Holy Spirit has made you overseers, to shepherd the church of God which He purchased with His own blood."

A fourth term, *agrypneō*, means "to keep alert" or "to stay awake."[13] Twice in the Gospels, Jesus urges His disciples to stay awake in view of the coming of the Son of Man (Mark 13:33; Luke 21:36). After his call to put on the whole armor of God in Ephesians 6, Paul uses this word to describe the armor-clad believer's posture in prayer: "praying always with all prayer and supplication in the Spirit, being *watchful* to this end with all perseverance and supplication for all the saints"

---

12. W. Arndt, F. W. Danker, and W. Bauer, *A Greek-English Lexicon of the New Testament and Other Early Christian Literature*, 3rd ed. (Chicago: University of Chicago Press, 2000), 880. Used twenty-four times in the New Testament, this word could be translated "beware" or "pay attention."

13. *Agrypneō* is used four times in the New Testament, each time in a moral sense.

(v. 18). Hebrews 13:17 describes the responsibilities of leaders over the church: "Obey those who rule over you, and be submissive, for they *watch out* for your souls, as those who must give account. Let them do so with joy and not with grief, for that would be unprofitable for you."

There is also the word *skopeō*, from which we get the word "scope," as in periscope, telescope, and microscope. This word means "to look out for" and is used in Galatians 6:1: "Brethren, if a man is overtaken in any trespass, you who are spiritual restore such a one in a spirit of gentleness, *considering* yourself lest you also be tempted."

The final word, *epechō*, means "to hold fast to something." This is the word Paul uses in his exhortation to young Timothy: "*Take heed* to yourself and to the doctrine. Continue in them, for in doing this you will save both yourself and those who hear you" (1 Tim. 4:16).

The Ingredients of Watchfulness

Taken together, these words in their biblical contexts suggest four essential ingredients to the practice of watching: wakefulness, attentiveness, vigilance, and expectancy.

Wakefulness

When I was eighteen, I fell asleep at the wheel. My dad was preaching at a church two hundred miles from the farm where we lived in Tokio, Texas. We left early enough that morning to make the three-hour drive and arrive before the hymns began. I was driving while Dad went over notes for his sermon, prayed, and took a brief nap.

We both woke up at the same time, as the minivan careened right, then bounced along the wide shoulder of the straight (and mercifully empty) Texas highway.

Both of us were startled.

No one was hurt.

I've never forgotten the experience, and two decades later I'm more cautious, more wakeful, and more alert to the danger of drowsiness—especially when my family of six makes the long trek from Indiana to Texas or Georgia to visit family. I'll do anything to stay awake: Roll down a window. Chew straws. Eat sunflower seeds. Drink absurd amounts of caffeine. Slap myself in the face. The frightening realization that my vehicle, traveling the interstate at seventy miles an hour, is only a few careless seconds away from a fatal collision makes me vigilant. As long as I'm behind the wheel, sleep is not an option.

Watchfulness demands wakefulness. If the eyes are shut in slumber, they are not open for observation. You cannot be alert and asleep at the same time. When Jesus told His disciples to watch and pray with Him for one hour, He was telling them to stay awake. There is, therefore, a physical dimension to this discipline.

In *The Christian in Complete Armour*, William Gurnall explains watching in both literal and metaphorical senses. "Watching, literally taken," he says, "is an affection of the body...a voluntary denying of our bodies sleep, that we may spend either the whole or part of the night in pious exercises."[14] As fasting is temporary abstinence from food, so watching is temporary abstinence from sleep. This is the sense

---

14. William Gurnall, *The Christian in Complete Armour* (1845; repr., Edinburgh: Banner of Truth Trust, 1964), 2:499.

Puritan Definitions of Watchfulness

In their experimental treatises, practical sermons, and manuals of casuistry, the Puritans frequently exhorted believers to practice watchfulness.

This potpourri of Puritan quotations shows both the variety and similarity in their working definitions of this crucial spiritual discipline.

> John Downame: "Watchfulness of the soul is when we do not sleep in our sins, being rocked in the cradle of carnal security, but shake off our drowsiness by unfeigned repentance, rising up to newness of life."[a]

> Richard Sibbes: "'Watching' is when upon waking all the powers and graces are in exercise, preparing for good and avoiding of evil."[b]

> Thomas Brooks: "Watchfulness includes a waking, a rousing up of the soul. It is a continual, careful observing of our hearts and ways, in all the turnings of our lives, that we still keep close to God and his word."[c]

> Isaac Ambrose: "Watchfulness is the first and principle help to all exercises of religion; it is the eye to see them all well done and used, and therefore we set it in the front of all duties…. For the nature

of it: 'Watchfulness is a continual, careful observing of our ways in all the passages and turnings of
our life, that we still keep close to the written word
of God.'"[d]

Thomas Boston: "Watching is a military term....
There are two things in it: 1. The soul's keeping spiritually awake, for to watch is opposed to
sleeping.... 2. Observation.... Our mind must be
intent upon our business, that we may catch all
advantages against, and ward off hazard from the
enemy. Hence watching is expressed by taking
heed, and by looking to ourselves (1 Cor. 10:12;
2 John 8)."[e]

---

a. John Downame, *The Christian Warfare* (London: William Stansby,
1634), 28.

b. Richard Sibbes, "The Christian's Watch," in *The Works of Richard
Sibbes*, ed. Alexander B. Grosart (1862; repr., Edinburgh: Banner of Truth
Trust, 2001), 7:299.

c. Thomas Brooks, *Precious Remedies against Satan's Devices*, in *The
Works of Thomas Brooks*, ed. Alexander B. Grosart (1866; repr., Edinburgh:
Banner of Truth Trust, 2001), 1:160.

d. Isaac Ambrose, Prima, Media, et Ultima, *Or, The First, Middle, and
Last Things* (Glasgow: James Knox, 1804), 119–20. Ambrose had obviously
read Brooks since he quotes him here.

e. Thomas Boston, "Christian Watchfulness Stated, and Enforced,"
in *The Whole Works of Thomas Boston*, ed. Samuel M'Millen (Aberdeen:
George and Robert King, St. Nicholas Street, 1848), 4:387–88.

in which Paul lists "watchings" among his ministerial creden-
tials in 2 Corinthians 6:5: "in stripes, in imprisonments, in
tumults, in labours, in watchings, in fastings" (KJV).

We also see the literal aspect of watchfulness in David's
earnest pursuit of God in Psalm 63:6: "When I remember
You on my bed, I meditate on You in the night watches." The
psalmists compare themselves to sentinels, entrusted with
guarding the city through the long, lonely vigils of night. So
we read in Psalm 130:6:

> My soul waits for the Lord
> More than those who watch for the morning—
> Yes, more than those who watch for the morning.

And in Psalm 119:148: "My eyes are awake through the night
watches, that I may meditate on Your word."

Jesus Himself observed such vigils, either praying long
into the night or rising before dawn to meet with God (Luke
6:12; cf. Mark 1:35), and believers should sometimes do the
same. As Gurnall says, "No doubt, for a devout soul, upon
some extraordinary occasions—so superstition be avoided
and health regarded—thus to watch unto prayer is not only
laudable but delectable."[15]

But wakefulness in Scripture is more often a picture for
mental and spiritual watchfulness. Gurnall observes, "Watching is taken metaphorically for the [vigilance] or watchfulness
of the soul," and, in this sense, watching "is not a temporary
duty," but the urgent and ongoing posture of one's life.[16] We
see this in Romans 13:11, where the apostle Paul reminds

---

15. Gurnall, *Christian in Complete Armour*, 2:499.
16. Gurnall, *Christian in Complete Armour*, 2:499, 500. John Downame
makes a similar distinction in *The Christian Warfare*:

believers that the hour has come for them to awake from
their sleep. But he is not rebuking them for taking a nap. Paul
isn't against Christians getting their seven hours of sleep or
catching a few Z's on a Saturday afternoon. Siestas are not a
necessary hindrance to one's sanctification. No, Paul writes
about spiritual slumber. He seeks to rouse his Roman friends
from the moral stupor of sin. Here are his words in full:

> And do this, knowing the time, that now it is high time
> to awake out of sleep; for now our salvation is nearer
> than when we first believed. The night is far spent, the
> day is at hand. Therefore let us cast off the works of
> darkness, and let us put on the armor of light. Let us
> walk properly, as in the day, not in revelry and drunken-
> ness, not in lewdness and lust, not in strife and envy.
> But put on the Lord Jesus Christ, and make no provi-
> sion for the flesh, to fulfill its lusts. (Rom. 13:11–14)

Notice the reason for his exhortation. "Awake out of
sleep," he says, "for now our salvation is nearer than when we
first believed." Paul was writing to people who were already
believers, so why did he refer to salvation as something yet to

---

Now this our watchfulness is partly of the body, and partly of the
soul. The bodily watching is the abstaining from natural sleep,
to the end that we may give ourselves unto prayer; when as with
David we water our couch with tears (Ps. 6:6), and call upon God
not only in the day, but in the night also (Ps. 88:1). And when as
even at midnight we rouse up ourselves to give thanks unto God for
his mercy and benefits (Ps. 119:61). The watchfulness of the soul is
when we do not sleep in our sins, being rocked in the cradle of carnal security, but shake off our drowsiness by unfeigned repentance,
rising up to newness of life. And to this watchfulness the Apostle
exhorteth us, Eph. 5:14: "Awake thou that sleepest, and stand up
from the dead, and Christ shall give thee light." *Christian Warfare*
(London: William Stansby, 1634), 28.

be obtained? When most of us talk about salvation, we refer to
something in the past, something that has already happened
to us. Sometimes the Scriptures do this too. Paul elsewhere
teaches that we have already been saved by grace through faith
(Eph. 2:8). But sometimes the Bible views salvation as a future
event. So, here. This salvation is a deliverance we have not yet
experienced, a rescue we are still waiting for. And this future
salvation is nearer to us now than when we first believed.

Romans 13:12 clarifies and extends the analogy: "The
night is far spent, the day is at hand." The day Paul has in
mind is the day of the Lord, the final, eschatological day,
the great day of salvation and judgment—salvation for the
church, judgment and wrath for the unbelieving, disobedient
world. Paul writes with a two-age schema in mind, viewing
human history in terms of two eras, the present age and the
age to come. The present age is the night, the age of darkness.
The age to come is the day, the age of life and light. Believers
live in the overlap of the ages. We are children of the future
day, children of the light, and yet we live in the present age
of darkness, the age of night. But since we are children of the
light, we are to "cast off the works of darkness, and…put on
the armor of light." We are to throw off the nightclothes and
get dressed for the dawning day.

Paul also used this schema in writing to the Thessalonians when he addressed believers who knew that the day of
the Lord would come like "a thief in the night" (1 Thess. 5:2).
Though this day will surprise the spiritually unprepared, who
vainly assure themselves of peace and security, believers will
not be surprised: "But you, brethren, are not in darkness, so
that this Day should overtake you as a thief. You are all sons

of light and sons of the day. We are not of the night nor of darkness" (1 Thess. 5:4–5). How, then, should we live?

> Therefore let us not sleep, as others do, but let us watch and be sober. For those who sleep, sleep at night, and those who get drunk are drunk at night. But let us who are of the day be sober, putting on the breastplate of faith and love, and as a helmet the hope of salvation. (1 Thess. 5:6–8)

This is the sobriety, the alertness, and the wakefulness to which we are called. As people who belong to the day, we must be mentally sober and morally alert, dressed in the Christian armor of faith, hope, and love. To be watchful is to be wakeful.

Attentiveness

Watchfulness also requires attentiveness. To watch is to consider, to notice, and to be on the alert. To watch is to pay attention. We should be like paratroopers training for a night drop behind enemy lines—attentive to both our mental and physical readiness for the mission and the instructions of our commanding officer. But all too often we're like passengers in coach on a commercial plane, quick to tune out the flight attendant's obligatory instructions before takeoff. We've heard it all before. The dangers seem neither urgent nor real. And the spy thriller we're reading is so much more interesting!

But both Jesus and the apostles demand our attentiveness. First, we must pay attention to the word of God. As Jesus tells His disciples, we are to "take heed," or pay attention, to what we hear. This exhortation follows the famous parable of the soils (Mark 4:3–20). In this parable Jesus uses different kinds of soil to illustrate the various ways people respond to the proclamation of the word. The parable itself is given in verses 3–9 while the interpretation follows in verses 13–20.

The meaning of this parable is straightforward. The seed represents the preaching of the word: the proclamation of the gospel, the good news of God's kingdom (cf. Mark 1:14; 2:2). The soils represent different kinds of hearers. Of the various soils, only one type was good: the soil that bore fruit. The other soils represent defective hearers and illustrate how our spiritual enemy, persecution, and worldliness can keep us from rightly receiving and responding to the word. "Good soil" hearers, in contrast, are described as those who hear the word, accept the word, and bear fruit. In this context Jesus says, "Take heed what you hear." The implication is that by failing to give full attention to the word, we can easily lose it. The enemy can snatch the word from our hearts. The word can wither in the burning heat of suffering, or it can be crowded out by worldly cares and desires.

Hebrews also emphasizes the importance of paying attention to the gospel: "Therefore we must give the more earnest heed to the things we have heard, lest we drift away" (Heb. 2:1). While this passage exhorts us to give careful heed to the word, the danger is pictured differently. Jesus's parable uses the agricultural language of seed and soil, but this text suggests a nautical illustration. Imagine a ship loosed from its moorings that imperceptibly drifts away from shore. That's the picture. This passage warns us against drifting from the gospel.[17]

---

17. In this context the author is addressing Jewish (Hebrew) believers who were being tempted to retreat from the gospel back to the old covenant. His letter is structured with a series of increasingly urgent exhortations to hold on to the gospel and persevere in it. These exhortations are buttressed with one of the richest explanations of the person and work of Christ in the New

We cannot pay careful attention to the gospel without at the same time paying attention to ourselves. Watchfulness involves considering our own hearts and ways. That's why Richard Rogers defines watchfulness as "a careful observing of our hearts, and diligent looking to our ways, that they may be pleasing, and acceptable unto God."[18]

Jesus often warned His disciples, urging them to "Take heed to *yourselves*" (Luke 17:3). In another passage He says,

---

Testament, as the author carefully showcases Christ's supremacy over angels, Moses, and the entire Levitical priesthood and sacrificial system of the old covenant. In his exposition of Hebrews, John Owen thus says: "To attend… unto the word preached, is to consider the *author* of it, the *matter* of it, the *weight* and *concernment* of it, the *ends* of it, with faith, subjection of spirit, and constancy, as we shall with our apostle more at large afterwards explain." *An Exposition of the Epistle to the Hebrews*, in *Works*, 20:261–62. In his further exposition of this verse, Owen says that five things are included in paying attention to the gospel word. First we need to *perceive the value of the grace* offered to us in the gospel. The more we value the word, the more careful attention we will give to it. "Constant high thoughts…of the necessity, worth, glory…excellency of the gospel, [and] especially of the author of it, and the grace dispensed in it, is the first step in that diligent heeding of it," Owen writes. The second ingredient is our *diligent study* of the word. "Diligent, sedulous searching into the word belongs unto this heeding of it, Ps. 1:2; or a laboring by all appointed means to become acquainted with it, wise in the mystery of it, and skilled in its doctrine." Third, the word will not profit us unless it is *mixed with faith*. "This is the life of heeding the word, without which all other exercise about it is but a dead carcass. To hear and not believe, is in the spiritual life what to see meat and not to eat is in the natural; it will please the fancy, but will never nourish the soul." Fourth, we should also labor to *express the word, by conforming our hearts and lives to it*. "When the heart of the hearer is quickened, enlivened, spirited with gospel truths, and by them is molded and fashioned into their likeness, and expresseth that likeness in its fruits…then is the word attended unto in a right manner." Last, paying careful attention to the word involves *watching against every opposition made against the truth or power of the word in us*. Since these oppositions are many, this "watchfulness should be great and diligent." Summarized from Owen, *Hebrews*, in *Works*, 20:264–66.

18. Rogers, *Holy Helps*, 41.

"But take heed to yourselves, lest your hearts be weighed down
with carousing, drunkenness, and cares of this life" (Luke
21:34). Pay attention to the word, and take heed to yourself.
In his first letter to Timothy, Paul joins these two objects of
watchfulness, exhorting his son in the faith to watch both his
private life and his public teaching: "Take heed to yourself
and to the doctrine. Continue in them, for in doing this you
will save both yourself and those who hear you" (1 Tim. 4:16).

But watchfulness especially means attentiveness to Christ
Himself. The only way to run the race before us is by "looking
unto Jesus, the author and finisher of our faith" (Heb. 12:2).
In his treatise *The Nature and Causes of Apostasy*, Owen prescribes watchfulness as one of the primary means of preserving
ourselves from apostasy.[19] In Owen's understanding, this watchfulness involves three kinds of attentiveness: (1) We must keep
the heart "awake and attentive unto its own deceitfulness."
(2) "We must keep our heart awake and attentive unto its help
and relief; and this lies only in Christ Jesus, the captain of our
salvation." (3) We must keep our heart "attentive unto its own
frames, its progress or decay in holiness."[20]

---

19. "Those who would be preserved in such a season *must keep a due and
careful watch over their own hearts* with respect unto their duty and danger: for
although temptations do abound, and those attended with all sorts of circumstances increasing their efficacy, and the outward means and causes of this evil
are multiplied, yet the beginnings of all men's spiritual declensions are in their
own hearts and spirits; for the different effects that these things have upon the
minds and lives of men is principally from themselves. As they are careful, diligent, and watchful over themselves in a way of duty on the one hand, or slothful,
careless, negligent on the other, so are they preserved or prevailed against."
Owen, *The Nature and Causes of Apostasy from the Gospel*, in *Works*, 7:245.

20. Owen, *Nature and Causes of Apostasy*, in *Works*, 7:247–48.

In chapter 3 we will discuss in more detail how to cultivate watchfulness over our hearts. But, dear Christian, don't miss the Christ-centeredness of Owen's approach. It is never sufficient to keep a close watch only on ourselves. Our eyes must be Christward. Only Christ can keep us from temptation (Rev. 3:10). When we fail to look "for all spiritual help and relief from Christ, for daily supplies of grace and strength from him alone,"[21] we are sure to fall.

Vigilance

One summer I worked for an old Texas rancher, killing mesquite trees on vast acres of uncultivated grassland. With a tank of Roundup on my back and a sprayer in my hand, I walked countless miles through the tall grass of these pastures. It was a boring job except for one thing: rattlesnakes.

I was in the Texas Big Country, an area famous for its annual Rattlesnake Roundup. My one measure of protection was a pair of plastic chaps, hard enough to deflect the fangs of a rattler, worn over my jeans. But the chaps weren't enough to take me off my guard. Like my childhood hero Indiana Jones, I *hated* snakes (still do)! And I never knew when a rattler would cross my path. One time I came within about two feet of stepping on one! That made me vigilant. I watched where I

---

21. Owen, *Nature and Causes of Apostasy*, in *Works*, 7:248. Consider also the words of Elvina M. Hall's old hymn "Jesus Paid It All" (1865, in the public domain):

> I hear the Savior say,
> "Thy strength indeed is small,
> Child of weakness, watch and pray,
> Find in Me thine all in all."

stepped. I listened for any faint hint of a rattle. And I jumped at any sudden movements.

Vigilance is the third component of watchfulness. The word *vigilance* adds something to wakefulness and attentiveness. It adds the element of danger. To be vigilant is to be on guard. The sentinel of a city is vigilant. He watches for the approach of the enemy. Warriors are vigilant. They are watchful and wary of their antagonist's every move. People become vigilant when they realize they are in jeopardy.

As soldiers of the cross, we are surrounded by enemies. In the words of an old hymn:

> Christian, seek not yet repose,
> Cast thy dreams of ease away;
> Thou art in the midst of foes:
> Watch and pray.

Who are these lethal foes that surround us? For centuries the Christian church, summarizing the teaching of Scripture, has given a threefold answer: the world, the flesh, and the devil.[22]

Our first foe is the world. Scripture warns, "Do not love the world or the things in the world. If anyone loves the world, the love of the Father is not in him. For all that is in the world—the lust of the flesh, the lust of the eyes, and the pride of life—is not of the Father but is of the world. And the world is passing away, and the lust of it; but he who does the

---

22. See especially Downame's *Christian Warfare*. As a portion of the fuller title suggests, Downame's entire book is structured around this trilogy of foes: *The Christian Warfare, wherein is first generally showed the malice, power, and politic strategems of the spiritual enemies of our salvation, Satan and his assistants the world and the flesh; with the means also whereby the Christian may withstand and defeat them.*

will of God abides forever" (1 John 2:15–17). James says that
friends of the world make themselves God's enemies (James
4:4). The world, in these passages, refers to the rebellion of
human beings against God expressed in desires and ambitions
aligned against the Father's will.

The second foe hangs its helmet in our own hearts. It
is the enemy of indwelling sin, or what Paul often calls the
"flesh." For example, in Romans 7:18–20 we read:

> For I know that in me (that is, in my flesh) nothing
> good dwells; for to will is present with me, but how to
> perform what is good I do not find. For the good that
> I will to do, I do not do; but the evil I will not to do,
> that I practice. Now if I do what I will not to do, it is no
> longer I who do it, but sin that dwells in me.

We are given a similar picture in Galatians 5:

> I say then: Walk in the Spirit, and you shall not fulfill
> the lust of the flesh. For the flesh lusts against the Spirit,
> and the Spirit against the flesh; and these are contrary
> to one another, so that you do not do the things that
> you wish…. And those who are Christ's have crucified
> the flesh with its passions and desires. (vv. 16–17, 24)

These passages, and many more, show that though believers "have crucified the flesh with its passions and desires"
(Gal. 5:24), their conflict with the flesh continues (Gal. 5:17).
We are always in danger of being seduced by the desires of the
flesh that bubble up from within. Like an undercover spy, sin
lurks in the corridors of our hearts and minds, watching for
any opportunity to betray us. "There remains in a regenerate
man a smoldering cinder of evil, from which desires continually leap forth to allure and spur him to commit sin," writes

Calvin.[23] This cinder can burst into flame at any time, in any place. That's why we need vigilance. As Paul commands, "Do not let sin reign in your mortal body, that you should obey it in its lusts" (Rom. 6:12). Peter agrees: "Beloved, I beg you as sojourners and pilgrims, abstain from fleshly lusts which war against the soul" (1 Peter 2:11).

Our third and greatest enemy is the ancient serpent, who is also "called the Devil and Satan, who deceives the whole world" (Rev. 12:9), and the spiritual forces of evil under his command (Eph. 6:12). I agree with C. S. Lewis, who says we must avoid two errors in our beliefs about demons: "One is to disbelieve in their existence. The other is to believe, and to feel an excessive and unhealthy interest in them."[24] In other words, while we shouldn't suspect demonic influence behind every flat tire or case of the flu, neither should we discount their real antagonism toward our spiritual well-being. In Peter's words, "Be sober, be vigilant; because your adversary the devil walks about like a roaring lion, seeking whom he may devour" (1 Peter 5:8).

Expectancy
The final ingredient of watchfulness is expectancy. If vigilance sounds the note of warning, then expectancy signals hope—not the flimsy hope of wishful thinking, but the confident expectation of promises fulfilled by a faithful God.

---

23. John Calvin, *Institutes of the Christian Religion*, ed. John T. McNeil, trans. Ford Lewis Battles (Philadelphia: Westminster, 1960), 3.3.10 (602).

24. C. S. Lewis, *The Screwtape Letters* (New York: HarperCollins, 2001), ix.

We see this in Psalm 130:5–8, where the psalmist likens himself to the city sentry on his night vigil, desperate for the breaking of dawn:

> I wait for the LORD, my soul waits,
> And in His word I do hope.
> My soul waits for the Lord
> More than those who watch for the morning—
> Yes, more than those who watch for the morning.
>
> O Israel, hope in the LORD;
> For with the LORD there is mercy,
> And with Him is abundant redemption.
> And He shall redeem Israel
> From all his iniquities.

The psalmist waits for the Lord and hopes in His word. According to Owen, his waiting is characterized by quietness, diligence, and expectation.[25] This is the posture of the watchful soul, preserving it from presumptuous haste, sinful sloth, and unbelieving despair. The watchman, sure that morning will come, sticks to his post through the long, dark night. And the believer, confident in God's word of promise, waits in hopeful expectation for the morning dawn of redemption.

We also hear the note of expectancy in Jesus's eschatological parable of the wise and foolish virgins in Matthew 25 (*eschatology* concerns the doctrine of last things). Do you remember the story? Jesus tells of ten virgins who go out to meet the bridegroom with lamps (or lanterns) in hand. The wise virgins bring oil for their lamps while the foolish do not. A cry heard at midnight signals the bridegroom's coming, but the foolish virgins find themselves with no oil. They leave to

---

25. John Owen, *An Exposition upon Psalm CXXX*, in *Works*, 6:611.

buy more but miss the bridegroom's arrival. Only the wise virgins are prepared. They are welcomed into the wedding feast while the foolish virgins are shut out. When they return, they say, "Lord, Lord, open to us!" But the bridegroom replies, "I do not know you" and refuses to admit them (Matt. 25:11–12). At the end of His parable, Jesus delivers the sting in the tale: "Watch therefore, for you know neither the day nor the hour in which the Son of Man is coming" (v. 13).

This parable is instructive in how it places watchfulness in an eschatological framework and focuses our watch on Christ, the coming Son of Man. This is a common thread through the New Testament, running from the Gospels, through the Epistles, into the book of Revelation. As Jesus says in Luke 21:34: "But take heed to [or watch, ESV] yourselves, lest your hearts be weighed down with carousing, drunkenness, and cares of this life, and that Day come on you unexpectedly." Similarly, Peter writes, "But the end of all things is at hand; therefore be serious and watchful in your prayers" (1 Peter 4:7). And in Revelation 16:15 Christ says, "Behold, I am coming as a thief. Blessed is he who watches, and keeps his garments, lest he walk naked and they see his shame."

When framed in its eschatological context, watchfulness has a twofold function: to keep us in a constant state of readiness and to focus our sights on Christ. So while watchfulness requires our moral vigilance, it does not consist in our sanctified navel gazing but in fixing our eyes on Jesus and seeing everything else in the glorious light of His past triumph and future coming. Far from being gloomy, watchful Christians are thus the most hopeful people of all. Their whole lives are vibrant with joyful expectancy for the Bridegroom's return.

Watch and Pray

Watchfulness, then, consists of four essential ingredients: wakefulness, attentiveness, vigilance, and expectancy. Watching involves staying awake both morally and spiritually; paying attention to God's word, to our own souls, and especially to Christ Himself; maintaining vigilance against our mortal enemies: the world, the flesh, and the devil; and hoping in the Lord—in His promises and His return.

I conclude this chapter with the words of a nineteenth-century British poet, Charlotte Elliot, whose hymn "Christian, Seek Not Yet Repose" captures the essential nature of watchfulness. I have already quoted the first verse, but here are the rest of the verses. Read and heed.

> Principalities and powers,
> Mustering their unseen array,
> Wait for thy unguarded hours:
> Watch and pray.
>
> Gird thy heavenly armor on,
> Wear it ever, night and day;
> Ambushed lies the evil one:
> Watch and pray.
>
> Hear the victors who o'ercame;
> Still they mark each warrior's way;
> All with one sweet voice exclaim,
> "Watch and pray."
>
> Hear, above all, hear Thy Lord,
> Him thou lovest to obey;
> Hide within thy heart His word,
> "Watch and pray."

> Watch, as if on that alone
> Hung the issue of the day;
> Pray that help may be sent down:
> Watch and pray.[26]

Examine and Apply

1. The Christian life is a journey, a race, and a battle; you are a pilgrim, an athlete, and a soldier. Which of these metaphors has most informed your understanding of the Christian life? Why?

2. Read and meditate on Owen's definition of watchfulness. Which aspects of watchfulness are missing from your life?

3. Consider reading through the New Testament letters, marking every occurrence of the words "watch," "take heed," and "pay attention," and others expressing this idea. Write down any new insights you gain from this study.

4. What are the four ingredients of watchfulness?

5. Are you exercising vigilance against the world, the flesh, and the devil, or have you let down your

---

26. Charlotte Elliot, "Christian, Seek Not Yet Repose" (1836), in the public domain.

guard? Ask the Lord to show you where renewed watchfulness is most needed in your life.

6. How often do you think about Christ's return? How should the hope of the second coming make you both more watchful and more joyful?

Chapter 2

Why?
The Necessity of Watchfulness

> There is need of great care, heedfulness, watchfulness,
> and circumspection, for a due continuance in our pro-
> fession, to the glory of God and advantage of our own
> souls. A careless profession will issue in apostasy open
> or secret, or great distress.... Our course is a warfare:
> and those who take not heed, who are not circumspect
> in war, will assuredly be a prey to their enemies.
>
> —John Owen, *An Exposition of the*
> *Epistle to the Hebrews*

This much is already clear: watchfulness requires effort. We
are pilgrims on a cross-country trek across dangerous, enemy-
occupied territory. The journey before us is long, grueling,
and filled with dangers. As runners in the heavenly race, we
are called to lay aside anything that will impede our progress.
This demands discipline and holy sweat. And like soldiers,
we battle in the Spartan conditions common to any war. The
stakes are high, and our enemies fierce.

I can understand, then, if this sketch of watchfulness
doesn't sound particularly inviting. As the early Puritan Richard Rogers observed, "Watchfulness is counted too strict until

people are well acquainted with it."[1] Rogers himself learned
the necessity of watching through the experience of defeat.
As a young man, he was troubled by his hardness of heart and
his inability to quickly pull himself out of spiritual lethargy.
Sometimes he would find himself unfit for spiritual duties for
hours or even days.[2] But by practicing watchfulness, Rogers
developed such constancy in his walk with God that he was
later called "the Enoch of his age."[3]

If you find the thought of watchfulness too strict, this
chapter is for you. Sure, watching takes effort. It will cost you
something. But this only underscores the value, necessity, and
urgency of this spiritual discipline. For in truth, while watchfulness will cost you something, *not* watching will cost you
more. Why is watching necessary? Consider seven reasons.

The Value of the Heart
Watchfulness is needful because the heart is valuable. According to A. W. Pink, keeping the heart is "the great task which

1. Rogers, *Holy Helps*, 47.
2. Consider this December 22, 1587, diary entry:

And I had this meditation one morning that, comparing this course
in which view my life continually, with the former wherein I did it by
fits and thus was oft unsettled, out of order, and then either not seeing
myself, though I had been unwatchful, walked in great danger by every
occasion, or, seeing could not easily recover myself, and so went unfit,
many hours and sometime days, for my calling, sometime dumpish and
too heavy, sometime loose, and many such fruits following, as no study,
but unprofitableness, I saw an unmeasurable difference, and said with
myself that as this was the life of a Christian so desired that it might
ever be my companion.

Richard Rogers and Samuel Ward, *Two Elizabethan Puritan Diaries*, ed. M. M.
Knappen (Chicago: American Society of Church History, 1933), 70.
3. Joel Beeke and Randall J. Pederson, *Meet the Puritans: With a Guide to
Modern Reprints* (Grand Rapids: Reformation Heritage Books, 2007), 507.

God has assigned unto each of His children."[4] In the words of Solomon: "Keep your heart with all diligence, for out of it spring the issues of life" (Prov. 4:23). Solomon is not talking about the blood-pumping organ in your chest, but the control center of your life. He is talking about your soul.

Your heart, or your soul (the biblical words are synonymous), is the most important part of you. It is command central. It is the seat of your thoughts, affections, and desires. In *The Holy War* John Bunyan pictures the heart as the central palace in the city of Mansoul:

> There was reared up in the midst of this town a most famous and stately palace; for strength, it may be called a castle; for pleasantness, a paradise; for largeness, a place so copious as to contain all the world. This place, the King Shaddai intended but for himself alone, and not another with him.... This place Shaddai made also a garrison of, but committed the keeping of it only to the men of the town.[5]

Jesus said the soul is more valuable than the world: "What profit is it to a man if he gains the whole world, and loses his own soul? Or what will a man give in exchange for his soul?" (Matt. 16:26). He also taught that your words and deeds flow from this central part of your being: "Out of the abundance of the heart the mouth speaks" (Matt. 12:34). Who you are in your heart is who you are. The various streams of your life flow from the fountain of your heart. If your heart is not watched, then your life will be a mess.

---

4. A. W. Pink, *Guarding Your Heart* (Pensacola, Fla.: Chapel Library, 2010), 9.
5. John Bunyan, *The Holy War* (Ross-shire, Scotland: Christian Focus, 1993), 20.

The problem is that our hearts have become sick, diseased by the deadly contagion of sin. In the words of the prophet Jeremiah:

> The heart is deceitful above all things,
> And desperately wicked;
> Who can know it? (Jer. 17:9)

Until purified by God's cleansing power and changed by God's transforming grace, our hearts are incapable of true godliness. The good news for believers is that God *has*, in fact, changed our hearts: "For it is the God who commanded light to shine out of darkness, who has shone in our hearts to give the light of the knowledge of the glory of God in the face of Jesus Christ" (2 Cor. 4:6). Into the darkness of our benighted minds, God brings light. Into the chaos of our inner worlds, He brings order. The Lord of new creation speaks the words of life and light to our dead, darkened souls. He cleanses our hearts through faith (Acts 15:9).

But even after new birth, our hearts must be kept. They must be guarded from fleshly desires that wage a relentless guerrilla warfare against our souls (1 Peter 2:11). Sin's dominion over us is broken, but its seditious influence remains. The heart must be watched, for "the heart hath a thousand wiles and deceits."[6] Sin still dwells within.

In his book *Soul Keeping*, John Ortberg compares the soul to a beautiful, crystal-clear stream high in the Alps that strengthened and refreshed a mountain village. The stream was fed by mountain springs, which were tended by an old

---

6. Owen, *The Nature, Power, Deceit, and Prevalency of the Remainders of Indwelling Sin in Believers*, in *Works*, 6:175.

man called the Keeper of the Springs. His job was to remove branches, leaves, and other debris from the springs, lest they pollute the stream.

One year the village decided to fire the old man and spend their money elsewhere. With no one tending the springs, the water became polluted: "Twigs and branches and worse muddied the liquid flow. Mud and silt compacted the creek bed; farm wastes turned parts of the stream into stagnant bogs." Though no one noticed at first, eventually the village was affected. Some people got sick. Kids no longer played in the water. Its crisp scent and sparkling beauty were gone.

Finally, the council of the village reconvened and rehired the old man to clean up the springs. After a time, "the springs were cleaned, the stream was pure, children played again on its banks, illness was replaced by health…and the village came back to life." "The life of a village," Ortberg writes, "depended on the health of the stream."

Are you keeping your soul? Is your innermost soul a palace cleansed and prepared for the dwelling of the king? Are the thoughts, words, and behaviors flowing from your heart pure and refreshing? Or have you neglected your watch? "The stream is your soul. And you are the keeper."[7]

The Danger of a Hard Heart
Your heart is valuable, but it is always in danger of being hardened. Have you ever felt the Spirit's prompting to kneel in prayer, or reflect on Scripture, or write a generous check

---

7. John Ortberg, *Soul Keeping: Caring for the Most Important Part of You* (Grand Rapids: Zondervan, 2014), 13–14.

for someone in need—and ignored it? Instead, you decided to make a phone call, channel surf, or check email.

And then, after a short while, the spiritual impulse disappeared. The inclination to pray vanished. Your desire for God's word evaporated with the morning dew. The spirit of generosity? Gone.

What happened? Your heart was hardened. The heart's proneness to hardness is another reason why watchfulness is necessary: "Beware, brethren, lest there be in any of you an evil heart of unbelief in departing from the living God; but exhort one another daily, while it is called 'Today,' lest any of you be hardened through the deceitfulness of sin" (Heb. 3:12–13).

As we will see in chapter 5, this passage is an exhortation to mutual watchfulness. The responsibility to watch is not only for individuals but also for churches. For now, I simply want to emphasize the purpose of the exhortation. Once you see the parallelism of verses 12 and 13, the intent in the exhortation is clear.

Look at the verses again. Notice the underlined commands and the italicized purpose clauses:

> <u>Beware</u>…*lest there be in any of you an evil heart of unbelief* in departing from the living God;

> But <u>exhort one another</u> daily…*lest any of you be hardened* through the deceitfulness of sin.

The twofold command to "beware" and "exhort one another" presents both negative and positive aspects of mutual watchfulness. The two purpose clauses indicate that departing from the living God because of an evil, unbelieving heart is equivalent to being hardened by sin's deception. The point is this: without spiritual vigilance, our hearts default to unbelief. Unbelief always leads to departure. Sin deceives us, and our hearts are hardened. And we begin to drift away from the lover of our souls. Left unchecked, our hearts are soon impenetrable, calcified by sin.

In *The Pilgrim's Progress*, Christian meets a man locked in an iron cage. When Christian asks how the man came to be there, the despondent captive replies, "I left off to watch and be sober; I laid the reins upon the neck of my lusts; I sinned against the light of the Word, and the goodness of God; I have grieved the Spirit, and He is gone; I tempted the devil, and he is come to me; I have provoked God to anger, and He has left me; I have so hardened my heart, that I cannot repent."[8] This is a frightening description of apostasy: the fate of those who fall away from God.

Final apostasy is not possible for a regenerate Christian. God's faithfulness to His promises, Christ's intercession for His people, and the indwelling of the Spirit in our hearts guarantee the perseverance of the saints in faith and holiness. Though you are a born-again believer, you may grieve the Spirit through sin, but "He who has begun a good work in you will complete it until the day of Jesus Christ" (Phil. 1:6). But while God preserves us from final apostasy, He uses both the promises and warnings of Scripture as means to help us persevere. The command to watch is one of those means.

John Owen warns against "a dangerous hardness of heart, where the guilt of one sin makes not the soul watchful against another of another sort."[9] This is the problem with a hard

---

8. John Bunyan, *The Pilgrim's Progress* (1895; repr., Edinburgh: Banner of Truth Trust, 1977), 31–32.

9. Owen, *A Treatise of the Dominion of Sin and Grace*, in *Works*, 7:537.

The Path of Apostasy

Bunyan's famous allegory *The Pilgrim's Progress* is a master-piece of experiential theology that illustrates a true believer's journey through the dangers, toils, and snares of this world with the manifold temptations, setbacks, triumphs, defeats, retreats, and recoveries that mark our experience.

Bunyan's story is noteworthy not only for its characters but for its careful articulation of practical Christian doctrine by means of dialogue between characters. In a discussion with his companion Hopeful about the backsliding and apostasy of Temporary and Turnback, Christian describes the path of apostasy in nine frightening steps:

1. They draw off their thoughts, all that they may, from the remembrance of God, Death, and Judgment to come.

2. Then they cast off by degrees private duties, as Closet-Prayer, Curbing their Lusts, Watching, Sorrow for Sin, and the like.

3. Then they shun the company of lively and warm Christians.

4. After that they grow cold to public duty, as Hearing, Reading, Godly Conference, and the like.

5. Then they begin to pick holes, as we say, in the coats of some of the Godly, and that devilishly, that they may have a seeming color to throw Religion (for the sake of some infirmity they have spied in them) behind their backs.

6. Then they begin to adhere to, and associate themselves, with carnal, loose, and wanton men.

7. Then they give way to carnal and wanton discourses in secret; and glad are they if they can see such things in any that are counted honest, that they may the boldly do it through their Example.

8. After this, they begin to play with little Sins openly.

9. And then being hardened, they show themselves as they are. Thus being launched again into the gulf of misery, unless a Miracle of Grace prevent it, they everlastingly perish of their own deceivings.[a]

---

a. John Bunyan, *The Pilgrim's Progress* (1895; repr., Edinburgh: Banner of Truth Trust, 1977), 177–78.

heart: it makes us callous, insensitive to sin. In contrast, Owen says, "wherever the heart is tender, upon a surprisal into sin, it will not only watch against the returns thereof or relapses into it, but will be made diligent, heedful, and careful against all other sins whatever."[10] A watchful heart is a tender heart.[11]

One of the primary preventions of hard-heartedness is the fear of the Lord. We don't hear enough about the fear of the Lord today, but the Scriptures are steeped with it. In Proverbs 28:14 we read, "Happy is the man who is always reverent, but he who hardens his heart will fall into calamity." Paul writes: "Therefore, having these promises, beloved, let us cleanse ourselves from all filthiness of the flesh and spirit, perfecting holiness in the fear of God" (2 Cor. 7:1). Again, he says: "Therefore, my beloved, as you have always obeyed, not as in my presence only, but now much more in my absence, work out your own salvation with fear and trembling; for it is God who works in you both to will and to do for His good pleasure" (Phil. 2:12–13). Peter's first letter commands us to "conduct yourselves throughout the time of your stay here in fear" (1 Peter 1:17). And in Hebrews we are exhorted to "serve God acceptably with reverence and godly fear. For our God is a consuming fire" (12:28–29).

---

10. Owen, *Dominion of Sin and Grace*, in *Works*, 7:537.

11. Bunyan says, "A tender heart is a wakeful, watchful heart. It watches against sin in the soul, sin in the family, sin in the calling, sin in spiritual duties and performances, &c. It watches against Satan, against the world, against the flesh, &c. But now, when the heart is not tender, there is sleepiness, unwatchfulness, idleness, a suffering the heart, the family, and calling to be much defiled, spotted, and blemished with sin; for a hard heart departs from God, and turns aside in all these things." John Bunyan, *The Acceptable Sacrifice*, in *The Whole Works of John Bunyan*, ed. George Offor (London: Blackie and Son, Paternoster Row, 1862), 1:712.

These passages clearly show that believers should be motivated by the fear of the Lord. But our fear of God is different from the servile fear of those who do not know God as their Father. The believer's fear is the reverent, loving fear of a child for his father, not the servile terror of a tyrant's slave. Calvin makes this distinction in his *Institutes*: "The dread arising from unbelief" is "far different from believers' fear." The wicked may fear God's wrath but have no true reverence for God. Believers, on the other hand, having rested in God's pardon and grace, "fear offending God more than punishment, and are not troubled by fear of punishment, as if it hung over their necks."[12] That is why the apostle John writes, "There is no fear in love; but perfect love casts out fear, because fear involves torment. But he who fears has not been made perfect in love" (1 John 4:18). John does not contradict Peter and Paul. He rather describes servile fear, the fear of punishment, while Peter and Paul urge true reverence for God, a fear of God that is joined to faith.

But this kind of fear, the godly fear of the believing heart, does not make us careless. It makes us watchful. In his *Treatise on the Fear of God*, John Bunyan says:

> There flows from this godly fear, watchfulness.... It makes them watch their hearts, and take heed to them with all diligence, lest they should, by one or another of its flights, lead them to do that which in itself is wicked (Prov. 4:23; Heb. 12:15). It makes them watch, lest some temptation from hell should enter into their heart to the destroying of them (1 Pet. 5:8). It makes them watch their mouths, and keep them also...that they

---

12. Calvin, *Institutes*, 3.2.27 (573).

offend not with their tongue.... It makes them watch
over their ways, look well to their goings, and to make
straight steps for their feet (Ps. 39:1; Heb. 12:13). Thus
this godly fear puts the soul upon its watch, lest from
the heart within, or from the devil without, or from the
world, or some other temptation, something should surprise and overtake the child of God to defile him, or to
cause him to defile the ways of God, and so offend the
saints, open the mouths of men, and cause the enemy to
speak reproachfully of religion.... This grace of fear is
the softest and most tender of God's honor of any other
grace. It is that tender, sensible, and trembling grace,
that keepeth the soul upon its continual watch.[13]

Charles Wesley prayed for just such a heart in one of his
hymns. Make this your prayer as well:

> I want a principle within
> Of watchful, godly fear,
> A sensibility of sin,
> A pain to feel it near.
> I want the first approach to feel
> Of pride or wrong desire,
> To catch the wandering of my will,
> And quench the kindling fire.[14]

The Danger of Temptation

When Jesus found His disciples sleeping, He said, "Watch and
pray, lest you enter into temptation" (Matt. 26:41). Probably
no one has analyzed Jesus's words more carefully than John

---

13. John Bunyan, *A Treatise on the Fear of God*, in *Works*, 1:462–63, 489.
14. Charles Wesley, "I Want a Principle Within" (1749), in the public
domain.

Owen. I have already referred to his penetrating treatise *Of Temptation*, an extended meditation on the danger of temptation and Jesus's twofold command to watch and pray.

According to Owen, three things are required in watching against temptation. The first requirement is a sense of danger or, in Owen's words, "a clear, abiding apprehension of the great evil that there is in entering into temptation."[15] His first direction for watching, then, is this: "Always bear in mind the great danger that it is for any soul to enter into temptation."[16]

The problem is that most of us don't believe temptation is all that dangerous. We may say that sin is dangerous. But temptation? "Everybody is tempted," we reason. "Besides, it's not a sin to be tempted. Even Jesus was tempted." And the icing on the cake: "We're saved by grace, not works." If we can keep ourselves from open, scandalous, life-destroying sins, we'll be fine. We may not be as holy as Brother John, but hey, we're just ordinary Christians.

This faulty reasoning makes us careless rather than watchful. Such self-talk betrays naïveté in our understanding of sin and distortion in our doctrine of grace. Sin is dangerous because it leads to death. Sin separates the soul from God: "The soul who sins shall die" (Ezek. 18:4). It is not a sin to be tempted, but when we do not flee temptation, sin will follow in its wake. If we grasp this, we will not take it lightly. Instead, we will resist the devil (James 4:7; 1 Peter 5:9) and flee from sin (1 Cor. 6:18; 10:14; 1 Tim. 6:11; 2 Tim. 2:22). In Bunyan's

---

15. Owen, *Of Temptation*, in *Works*, 6:123.
16. Owen, *Of Temptation*, in *Works*, 6:123.

Holy War, when Diabolus assaults Mansoul, the first casualty of war is Captain Resistance.[17]

A casual, careless attitude about sin betrays a heart still grasped by sin's power. In contrast, a realistic perspective on sin that recognizes sin as rebellion against God's authority, transgression of God's law, and the death knell to life, joy, and peace will not treat temptation lightly. Temptation and sin, apart from watching and prayer, go together. The one leads to the other. "Let no man, then, pretend to fear sin that doth not fear temptation to it," writes Owen. "They are too nearly allied to be separated."[18] But if we can daily keep alive in our hearts an awareness of sin's great danger to our souls, if, as Owen says, "the heart be made tender and watchful here, half the work...is over."[19]

Second, watching against temptation involves a sense of our own helplessness. We must never forget that it is not in our own power to keep ourselves from temptation and sin. Scripture teaches this over and again. When Jesus prayed for His disciples on the night He was betrayed, He prayed that the Father would keep them (John 17:15). We "are kept by the power of God through faith for salvation," writes Peter (1 Peter 1:5). "Keep yourselves in the love of God," Jude commands in verse 21 of his epistle.

Here again is Owen:

> Christ prays his Father to keep us, and instructs us to pray that we be so kept. It is not, then, a thing in our own power. The ways of our entering into temptation

---

17. Bunyan, *Holy War*, 25.
18. Owen, *Of Temptation*, in *Works*, 6:123.
19. Owen, *Of Temptation*, in *Works*, 6:124.

are so many, various, and imperceptible,—the means of
it so efficacious and powerful,—the entrances of it so
deceitful, subtle, insensible, and plausible,—our weakness, our unwatchfulness, so unspeakable,—that we
cannot in the least keep or preserve ourselves from it.
We fail both in wisdom and power for this work.[20]

We need to be constantly reminded of both our weakness and
God's gracious compassion and His willingness to help us. The
Father invites us to come to His throne of grace in the time
of need. And our sympathetic High Priest, who was tempted
as one of us yet never once succumbed to sin, gives us confidence that we will be both heard and helped when we come.
Remembering our helplessness helps us to stay watchful.

Watchfulness also includes exercising faith in the promises of God. This is Owen's third requirement. Our faithful
covenant Father has promised to keep us. He has promised
a way of escape for tempted believers: "No temptation has
overtaken you except such as is common to man; but God is
faithful, who will not allow you to be tempted beyond what
you are able, but with the temptation will also make the way
of escape, that you may be able to bear it" (1 Cor. 10:13). This
promise is sure and steadfast.

But God intends for us to trust these promises. We are kept
for salvation by the power of God *through faith* (1 Peter 1:5).
And the way we depend on God's promise to keep us and
deliver us is to pray. Isn't this what Jesus taught? "In this
manner, therefore, pray…. Do not lead us into temptation,
but deliver us from the evil one" (Matt. 6:9, 13). In Owen's

---

20. Owen, *Of Temptation*, in *Works*, 6:125. I've slightly edited this quotation by updating archaic words with modern equivalents.

memorable words, "He that would be little in temptation, let him be much in prayer."[21]

Your Adversary, the Devil

Closely aligned with the danger of temptation is the tempter himself. But many believers underestimate the evil one's power to deceive. Evil sometimes feels more terrifying in fiction than in real life. People shudder at the description of malevolent aliens, vampires, and Black Riders but greet biblical warnings about the devil with a yawn. But though the Nazgûl in Tolkien's *Lord of the Rings* are truly frightening, the mortal enemy of our souls is more terrible by far. "Be sober, be vigilant," writes Peter, "because your adversary the devil walks about like a roaring lion, seeking whom he may devour" (1 Peter 5:8).

Listen up, Christian. You have an implacable enemy whose single objective is to plant a victory flag in the soil of your vanquished faith. He wants to devour you, consume you, and destroy you.

Writing to the Corinthians, Paul says, "We are not ignorant of his devices" (2 Cor. 2:11). Are you? Do you recognize the danger of his deceptions, the malignity of his temptations, and the subtlety of his insinuations? Don't underestimate the devil. As Richard Rogers observes, the devil first comes to us as a tempter and then as an accuser.[22] First he seduces us with the fleeting pleasures of sin. When he succeeds, he tallies up our transgressions and roars in our consciences in the hellish attempt to drive us to despair.

---

21. Owen, *Of Temptation*, in *Works*, 6:126.
22. Rogers, *Holy Helps*, 49.

Sometimes he even injects evil, blasphemous thoughts into our minds. There is a scene in *Pilgrim's Progress* where Christian passed through the Valley of the Shadow of Death and came to the mouth of a burning pit. Bunyan tells us that at just that moment, "one of the wicked ones got behind him, and stepped up softly to him, and, whisperingly, suggested many grievous blasphemies to him, which he verily thought had proceeded from his own mind."[23] A wise friend once told me that the enemy speaks to us in our own voice and with our own accent.[24]

The point is this: we have a spiritual enemy who is poised to make us fall any way he can.

> For still our ancient foe
> Doth seek to work us woe
> His craft and power are great
> And armed with cruel hate
> On earth is not his equal.[25]

Watchfulness is necessary because we are at war and the stakes are high. This is surely one reason why Paul includes watchfulness as he exhorts us to prayer, following his exposition of the Christian armor in Ephesians 6: "praying always with all prayer and supplication in the Spirit, being watchful to this end with all perseverance and supplication for all the saints" (v. 18).

This suggests that watching is one means for putting the armor on. As Rogers says, "To have this armor ready to keep

---

23. Bunyan, *Pilgrim's Progress*, 68.
24. Thanks to Laurie Kopf, who credits Ney Bailey with this quote.
25. Martin Luther, "A Mighty Fortress Is Our God" (1529), trans. Frederick H. Hedge (1852), in the public domain.

us and conduct us safely throughout our life in our practice of Christianity, this is to be done: we must watch continually and pray with heart (Matt. 26:41). This we must do often."[26]

The Assurance of Salvation

Watchfulness is also necessary as a means of maintaining our assurance of salvation. Now do not misunderstand: watchfulness does not justify us. The basis of our acceptance with God is our Lord Jesus Christ's righteous obedience, atoning death, and triumphant resurrection from the dead. We are justified by grace alone, through faith alone, in Christ alone. As Paul writes, Christ

> was delivered up because of our offenses, and was raised because of our justification.[27]
>
> Therefore, having been justified by faith, we have peace with God through our Lord Jesus Christ. (Rom. 4:25–5:1)

But justified believers can lose the assurance of their salvation through lack of watchfulness. For this reason Peter exhorts believers to be "diligent to make your call and election sure" (2 Peter 1:10).

Watchfulness is necessary for assurance because it is an essential part of our obedience and perseverance in faith and holiness. As we have already seen in this chapter, every believer is commanded to be watchful. The dangers of hardness of heart, the lures of temptation and sin, and the

---

26. Rogers, *Holy Helps*, 109.

27. Or better, "raised for our justification." The Greek word translated "because" is *dia*, a preposition indicating instrumentality or purpose. Paul seems to be saying that Christ's resurrection is the basis of our justification.

malignant threats of our adversary the devil demand our constant vigilance.

When believers lose assurance because of sin, renewing their watch is one of the means of getting back in the way of holiness and assurance. In his exposition of Psalm 130, a masterful treatment of forgiveness and assurance, Owen thus exhorts the doubting, struggling believer:

> Are you in depths and doubts, staggering and uncertain, not knowing what is your condition, nor whether you have any interest in the forgiveness that is of God? Are you tossed up and down between hopes and fears, and want peace, consolation and establishment? Why lie you upon your faces? Get up: watch, pray, fast, meditate, offer violence to your lusts and corruptions; fear not, startle not at their crying to be spared; press unto the throne of grace by prayer, supplications, importunities, restless requests—this is the way to take the kingdom of God. These are not peace, are not assurance, but they are part of the means God hath appointed for the attainment of them.[28]

Did you notice how Owen groups together a whole litany of spiritual disciplines? "Watch, pray, fast, meditate, offer violence to your lusts and corruptions," he writes. This sage advice is sure to help the Christian who applies it with faith in Christ and His promises.

The Gradual Onset of Spiritual Decay
A trip to the dentist brought bad news. I needed a root canal. An X-ray of a molar showed decay down to the nerve. It was

---

28. Owen, *An Exposition upon Psalm CXXX*, in *Works*, 6:567–68.

too late to simply fill the cavity. I had two choices: root canal or extraction.

I had noticed a problem, so I wasn't completely surprised. There were signs: food stuck in my teeth, irritation from cold water, an occasional toothache. But the problem began long before I noticed symptoms or received an official diagnosis. Decay sets in gradually, slowly, imperceptibly. The same is true in our spiritual lives.

Revelation 3 contains a letter to a group of Christians who had experienced spiritual decay. Delivered to the angel (or messenger) of the church through the apostle John, this is a personal letter from the exalted Christ to the church of Sardis. It is a letter of confrontation and exhortation, containing both diagnosis and cure.

> And to the angel of the church in Sardis write,
>
> "These things says He who has the seven Spirits of God and the seven stars: 'I know your works, that you have a name that you are alive, but you are dead. Be watchful, and strengthen the things which remain, that are ready to die, for I have not found your works perfect before God. Remember therefore how you have received and heard; hold fast and repent. Therefore if you will not watch, I will come upon you as a thief, and you will not know what hour I will come upon you.'" (Rev. 3:1–3)

The diagnosis is spiritual decay: "You have a name that you are alive, but you are dead" (v. 1). Here was a church with a good name. They had a reputation for spiritual vitality. By all outward appearances they were strong, active, and healthy. But the stench of death emits from beneath the floorboards of their religious activity. The good things that did remain in the church were ready to die. Their works were not perfect, or complete, before God (v. 2). They had contented themselves with half measures—partial obedience. They had a veneer of spirituality without the reality. They had the appearance of godliness but denied its power (2 Tim. 3:5).

We see the antidote to their spiritual malaise in a series of imperatives in verses 2–3: "be watchful," "strengthen the things which remain," "remember…how you have received and heard," "hold fast," and "repent." The cure for spiritual decay, in other words, is repentance, watchfulness, and renewed obedience.

Spiritual decay is dangerous because it is the beginning of apostasy. Spiritual decay is akin to what C. S. Lewis describes as "the safest road to Hell…the gentle slope, soft underfoot, without sudden turnings, without milestones, without signposts."[29] Because of God's preserving, persevering grace, true Christians cannot follow this road all the way to hell, but they can get miserably close and usually find the way back costly and painful.

What causes spiritual decay? Neglect. If you drink lots of soda, skimp on brushing your teeth, and skip flossing altogether, you can say hello to cavities. And if you soak up the world, skimp on Bible reading, skip meditation, and neglect your prayer life, you will soon be collecting your mail at the post office in Sardis.

There are many symptoms of spiritual decay. Here are two: going through the motions and cherishing a secret sin. To go through the motions is to read Scripture without applying it to your life, to sing hymns in church with little love for Jesus, and to mutter cold prayers with a heart far from God.

---

29. C. S. Lewis, *Screwtape Letters*, 72.

To cherish a secret sin is to persist in a deliberate pattern of ongoing disobedience, despite the warnings of conscience, the Holy Spirit, and the word, while pretending to others that everything is okay.

The cure for spiritual decay is renewed repentance and faith in Christ. And the prevention for spiritual decay? Watchfulness. Owen says that "most of our spiritual decays and barrenness arise from an inordinate admission of other things into our minds." This is what weakens "grace in all its operations."

> But when the mind is filled with thoughts of Christ and his glory, when the soul thereon cleaves unto him with intense affections, they will cast out, or not give admittance unto, those causes of spiritual weakness and indisposition.... Where we are engaged in this duty, it will stir up every grace unto its due exercise.... This will assuredly put us on a vigilant watch and constant conflict against all the deceitful workings of sin, against all the entrances of temptation, against all the ways and means of surprisals into foolish frames, by vain imaginations, which are the causes of our decays.[30]

Once again, we see the centrality of Christ in the whole business of watching. Only by keeping my mind "filled with thoughts of Christ and his glory" can I keep out the causes of spiritual weakness. Only by clinging to Jesus "with intense affections" will I watch against the catalysts to spiritual decay. And this leads to the most important motive for watching.

---

30. Owen, *Meditations and Discourses on the Glory of Christ Applied unto Unconverted Sinners and Saints Under Spiritual Decays*, in *Works*, 1:460–61.

The Sweetness of Fellowship with Christ

We've considered many reasons to watch in this chapter. Watching is needful because we are surrounded and assaulted by myriads of dangers. But the believer's deepest desire in watching is a positive one: to maintain fellowship with the Lord Jesus Christ.

Equally, the real key to watchfulness is staying close to the Lord. "Take heed of losing the liveliness and sweetness of your communion with God, lest thereby your hearts be loosed off from God," warns Flavel. "The heart is an hungry and restless thing; it will have something to feed upon; if it enjoy nothing from God, it will hunt for something among the creatures, and there it often loses itself, as well as its end. There is nothing more engages the heart to a constancy and evenness in walking with God, than the sweetness which it tastes therein."[31]

In *Of Communion with God the Father, Son, and Holy Ghost*, Owen considers this in his discussion of communion with the Son. Owen argues that there are certain affections that particularly suit our relationship to Christ as our bridegroom. The first of these affections is delight.[32] Using the spouse's experience in the Song of Songs as his template, Owen says that this delight is manifested in several ways. First, "by her exceeding *great care to keep his company* and society, when once she had obtained it."[33] The believer, like the chastened lover in Solomon's song, desires the Bridegroom's company above all

---

31. Flavel, *Saint Indeed*, in *Works*, 5:506.

32. "*The saints delight in Christ*; he is their joy, their crown, their rejoicing, their life, food, health, strength, desire, righteousness, salvation, blessedness: without him they have nothing; in him they shall find all things." Owen, *Of Communion with God the Father, Son, and Holy Ghost*, in *Works*, 2:124.

33. Owen, *Of Communion*, in *Works*, 2:125.

else. Owen observes, "The sum of her aim and desire is, that
nothing may fall out, nothing of sin or provocation happen,
that may occasion Christ to depart from her."[34] And it is this
aim that sets the believing soul upon its watch: "When once
the soul of a believer hath obtained sweet and real communion
with Christ, it looks about him, watcheth all temptations, all
ways whereby sin might approach, to disturb him in his enjoyment of his dear Lord and Saviour, his rest and desire. How
doth it charge itself not to omit anything, nor to do anything
that may interrupt the communion obtained!"[35] Notice how
this watchfulness is focused not just on avoiding temptations
and sins but against interrupting or disturbing the soul's enjoyment of Christ.

This, I confess, has sometimes been the missing element
in my own watchfulness. My concern has too often been to
merely keep my nose clean rather than to enjoy Christ. But
that is not true watchfulness. In fact, an indifference to enjoying Christ's fellowship reveals an already wandering heart. In
Owen's words, "*Carelessness* in the enjoyment of Christ pre-
tended, is a manifest evidence of a *false* heart."[36]

The next way the believer manifests delight in Christ is
"by the utmost impatience of his absence, with desires still of
nearer communion with him."[37] Owen drew this insight from
the spouse's cry in Song of Songs 8:6 (KJV): "Set me as a seal
upon thine heart, as a seal upon thine arm: for love is strong
as death; jealousy is cruel as the grave: the coals thereof

---

34. Owen, *Of Communion*, in *Works*, 2:126.
35. Owen, *Of Communion*, in *Works*, 2:126.
36. Owen, *Of Communion*, in *Works*, 2:126.
37. Owen, *Of Communion*, in *Works*, 2:126.

are coals of fire, which hath a most vehement flame." This describes the vehemence of the spouse's love, which cannot be satisfied apart from Christ's felt presence. While some scholars might quibble over Owen's interpretation of the Song of Songs, his description of the believer's ardent desire for Jesus rings true: "I am not able to bear the workings of love to thee, unless I may always have society and fellowship with thee. There is no satisfying of my love without it.... Death is not satisfied without its prey; if it have not all, it hath nothing.... So is my love; if I have thee not wholly, I have nothing."[38]

But what of those times when the believer has lost the sense of Christ's conscious smile? How does delight in Christ manifest itself then? Owen answers, "By her solicitousness, trouble, and *perplexity*, in his loss and withdrawings."[39] This is the third way the supreme desire for communion with Christ leads to watchfulness. Christ's absence leaves the soul troubled and perplexed.

Once more Owen drew his insights from the experience of the spouse in the Song of Songs, this time from 3:1–3:

> By night on my bed I sought the one I love;
> I sought him, but I did not find him.
> "I will rise now," I said,
> "And go about the city;
> In the streets and in the squares
> I will seek the one I love."
> I sought him, but I did not find him.
> The watchmen who go about the city found me;
> I said, "Have you seen the one I love?"

38. Owen, *Of Communion*, in *Works*, 2:127–28.
39. Owen, *Of Communion*, in *Works*, 2:128.

Owen's first comments after quoting this passage are as memorable as they are brief: "It is night now with the soul," he wrote, "a time of darkness and trouble, or affliction. *Whenever Christ is absent, it is night with a believer.*"[40] Don't move past this too quickly, dear Christian. Are you right now, at this moment, in fellowship with Christ? Are you conscious of His smile? Or does a dark shadow linger over your soul?

What must the believer do in the midnight of Christ's absence from the soul? Two things. "Seeking of Christ…hath two parts: searching of our own souls for the cause of his *absence*; secondly, searching the promises for his *presence.*"[41]

Seeking out the cause of Christ's absence requires self-examination. As we will see in chapter 3, this is an important aspect of watchfulness. But Owen was careful to maintain the relational framework within which this self-examination must take place. Sometimes we wrongly approach self-examination with the mentality of school children who must admit they broke the rules and then endure detention before being re-admitted to class. But our sins against Christ are not merely infractions against rules; they are spiritual adultery. That is why Owen teaches us to ask, "Where have I been wandering after other lovers?"[42]

But self-examination must be accompanied by expectant faith. We must not only inquire into the reasons for Christ's absence; we must also search for the promises of His restored presence. By laying hold of the promises, we embrace Christ

40. Owen, *Of Communion*, in *Works*, 2:128. Emphasis added.
41. Owen, *Of Communion*, in *Works*, 2:129.
42. Owen, *Of Communion*, in *Works*, 2:130.

Himself, as He comes to us "clothed with his gospel."[43] And by holding Him close, we imitate the spouse who, after finding the bridegroom, seized him and said, "I held him and would not let him go" (Song 3:4).

Examine and Apply

1. Read Proverbs 4:23. Why is the heart so central to the spiritual life?

2. This chapter focused on several threats to our spiritual lives that make watchfulness both necessary and urgent. What are these threats? What effect does considering these dangers have on you? Do you feel more vulnerable after reading this chapter?

3. You have an implacable enemy whose single objective is to plant a victory flag in the soil of your vanquished faith. He wants to devour you, consume you, destroy you. Has this made you more watchful, and in what way? What are some of Satan's most common strategies for tempting you? For further meditation, consider reading Thomas Brooks's helpful book *Precious Remedies against Satan's Devices*.

4. Do you ever struggle with a lack of assurance? Do you think neglecting watchfulness has played a role in your doubts?

---

43. This felicitous phrase is Calvin's from *Institutes*, 3.2.6 (548).

5. Think back to the most joyful, peaceful, fruitful times in your life as a Christian. What kinds of beliefs, affections, and habits characterized your life in those seasons? What has changed?

6. Spend some time in communion with Christ. Following Owen's counsel, seek out the causes of His absence and the promises of His presence. If you feel far from the Lord, ask Him to draw near to you and restore you to Himself.

Chapter 3

How?
The Cultivation of Watchfulness

Be sure to lay in provision in store against the approaching of any temptation. This also belongs to our
watchfulness over our hearts.... Gospel provisions will
do this work; that is, keep the heart full of a sense of the
love of God in Christ. This is the greatest preservative
against the power of temptation in the world.

—John Owen, *Of Temptation: The Nature and Power
of It; the Danger of Entering Into It;
and the Means of Preventing that Danger*

Now that the stakes are clear, it's time to get practical. It's
one thing to know you have a long journey ahead but quite
another to be prepared for the march. Deciding to run a
marathon is well and good. But if you don't train, your legs
will turn to marshmallows and you'll be kissing pavement.
And there is a vast difference between being enlisted in the
Marines and being prepared for active combat. That's what
boot camp is for.

So it is with watchfulness. It's not enough to know what
watchfulness is and that it's necessary; you must also be

equipped. You must also be trained. How, then, do you cultivate this discipline?

We have already seen hints at the answer, but there is
much more to learn from our Reformed and Puritan forebear-
ers. Since the material is both practical and rich, this is the
longest chapter in the book. Furthermore, I have chosen to be
more generous in this chapter with extended quotations from
Owen, Bunyan, M'Cheyne, and others. I've included these
nuggets of wisdom because they have been helpful to me. I
believe they will help you too.

We will look at nine strategies for cultivating watchfulness. As you work through these strategies, pause frequently
to prayerfully search your heart. Write down insights you find
helpful. My prayer is that you will emerge from this chapter
challenged, equipped, and encouraged.

Labor to Know Your Heart

"Nearly all the wisdom we possess," writes Calvin, "consists
in two parts: the knowledge of God and of ourselves.... We
cannot seriously aspire after him before we begin to become
displeased with ourselves."[1] Growth in this double knowledge
is the way the gospel works. The higher our vision of God's
majestic holiness, the deeper we perceive our own sinfulness.
The more we understand our weakness, the more we come to
rely on the strength of God's grace.

This is true in initial conversion. No one becomes a
Christian without recognizing their need for salvation and
the sufficiency of Christ to save. Diagnosis precedes cure. We
must "become displeased with ourselves" if we are to "seriously

---

1. Calvin, *Institutes*, 1.1.1 (35, 37).

aspire" to know Christ. We must reckon with our sin before we will seek the Savior.

But spiritual growth happens this way as well, and this is especially true in cultivating watchfulness. As we've already seen, watching requires moral and spiritual vigilance, alertness to the danger and deceitfulness of our spiritual enemies—the world, the flesh, and the devil. And since our enemies are not only external (the world and the devil) but also internal (the flesh), we must pay attention to ourselves.

In his first direction concerning the acts of watchfulness against temptation, Owen says: "Let him that would not enter into temptation labour to know his own heart, to be acquainted with his own spirit, his natural frame and temper, his lusts and corruptions, his natural, sinful, or spiritual weaknesses, that, finding where his weakness lies, he may be careful to keep at a distance from all occasions of sin."[2] The first step in practicing watchfulness, then, is to "consider your ways" (Haggai 1:5, 7). This is the discipline of regular self-examination.

Owen further breaks this down into two categories. First, we need a growing awareness of how our "natural tempers and constitutions"[3] make us susceptible to temptation and sin. The temptations of a laid-back, easy-going, phlegmatic person will be different from those of an ambitious, type A overachiever. Peter, with his bold and brash temperament, was more vulnerable to the sin of presumption while the naturally cynical Thomas struggled with doubt and unbelief. The melancholy prophets Elijah and Jonah were prone to discouragement and

---

2. Owen, *Of Temptation*, in *Works*, 6:131.
3. Owen, *Of Temptation*, in *Works*, 6:131.

depression. But Samson, the fierce warrior who judged Israel, and David, the passionate poet and mighty king, were easy prey to the lures of lust.

Your temperament leaves you more susceptible to some sins than others. Do you know yourself? Owen warns that "he who watches not this thoroughly, who is not exactly skilled in the knowledge of himself, will never be disentangled from one temptation or another all his days."[4]

We should also pay close attention to the "peculiar lusts or corruptions"[5] that have become firmly rooted in our hearts, what Isaac Ambrose calls "Delilah sins." Delilah sins, like Samson's Philistine mistress, like to sit on our laps and whisper sweet nothings in our ears, but they will betray us to our foes in a heartbeat and cut off our moral strength. Richard Rogers agrees: "We must especially watch against the infirmity which most annoys us."[6] These are the specific sin patterns we have cultivated through willful and habitual sin. Like deep ruts that furrow a muddy road, these vices are etched into our lives through daily routines, self-justifying rationalization, and continual repetition.

To change we must submit to the discipline of God's grace, which was secured through Christ, is applied by His Spirit, and now teaches us to deny ungodliness and worldly passions and "live soberly, righteously, and godly in the present age" (Titus 2:12). And following initial repentance, continual watchfulness is necessary. In Owen's words: "Labour to know thine own frame and temper; what spirit thou art of; what associates in

---

4. Owen, *Of Temptation*, in *Works*, 6:132.

5. Owen, *Of Temptation*, in *Works*, 6:132.

6. Rogers, *Holy Helps*, 55.

Delilah Sins

In Prima, Media, et Ultima, *Or, The First, Middle, and Last Things*, Isaac Ambrose gives detailed instructions for watchfulness over our sins (including original sin, actual sins, and special sins), hearts, tongues, and actions. His directions for watching over special sins—that is, "our Delilah sins, our darling delights"—are especially helpful. He prescribes seven rules:

1. Endeavour we the mortifying of this sin: some one sin there is in every soul of us that is most predominant. Now it is the main work of a Christian, as to fall out for ever with all sin, so especially to improve all his spiritual forces and aid from heaven, utterly to demolish, and to beat down to the ground this hold, this bosom-sin.

2. Lay we load of deepest groans, and strongest cries for mortifying grace against this domineering sin; especially every morning and evening strive with God in our prayers for a comfortable conquest over it....

3. Bend we ourselves against the special acts, occasions, and opportunities of this sin....

4. As oft as we find any motion of this sin to stir, and show itself in us, it will be convenient, not only to withhold our consent, but withal, to exercise some act of contrary holiness....

5. Settle we in ourselves a purpose of heart to forbear it for time to come: In undertaking of which purpose, it will be expedient to set ourselves some short space of time, in which we may force ourselves to the forbearance of it, as for a day, or a month, or the like: and when the prefixed time is come, we should then question ourselves, "How well we have performed? Or how, or wherein we have failed?" And then begin a new purpose, and prescribe ourselves a like time, for shunning of the same sin; and so on from time to time, till we have gotten a full victory.

6. If in our daily or monthly review we find that we have been defective in performing of what we have proposed, then with an holy revenge we should correct our former errors, beg pardon for our defects, and punish ourselves for such slothfulness, or willfulness, by abstinence from meat, ease, recreation (1 Cor. 9:27).... This holy revenge is commended by the apostle (2 Cor. 7:29) as a worthy fruit of serious repentance.

7. Above all, without which all the rest are nothing: believe the promises of pardon in the blood of Christ. It is faith in the promises which will be able to cleanse and purge the heart from this sin.[a]

---

a. Isaac Ambrose, Prima, Media, et Ultima, *Or, The First, Middle, and Last Things* (Glasgow: James Knox, 1804), 122–24.

thy heart Satan hath; where corruption is strong, where grace is weak; what stronghold lust hath in thy natural constitution, and the like.... Be acquainted, then, with thine own heart; though it be deep, search it; though it be dark, inquire into it, though it give all its distempers other names than what are their due, believe it not."[7] Such heart labor requires ruthless honesty in taking inventory of our lives. In the world of retail, no one particularly enjoys taking inventory. But every good manager knows that it is a crucial discipline for wise steward-ship. The same is true with us. Only by facing the truth about ourselves can we exercise vigilance at our points of weakness. This leads to a second direction for cultivating watchfulness.

Guard the Gates to Your Soul

To watch your life, you must guard your heart. And to guard your heart, you must persistently protect the points of entry to the heart. Bunyan refers to these entry points as five gates to the city of Mansoul: "Ear-gate, Eye-gate, Mouth-gate, Nose-gate, and Feel-gate."[8]

In like manner, Solomon's exhortation in Proverbs 4:23 to keep the heart is buttressed with direction for our ears, eyes, mouths, and feet. Notice how the italicized words correspond to Bunyan's gates:

> My son, give attention to my words;
> Incline your *ear* to my sayings.
> Do not let them depart from your *eyes*;
> Keep them in the midst of your heart;
> For they are life to those who find them,

---

7. Owen, *Of Temptation*, in *Works*, 6:132.
8. Bunyan, *Holy War*, 21.

And health to all their flesh.
Keep your heart with all diligence,
For out of it spring the issues of life.
Put away from you a deceitful *mouth*,
And put perverse *lips* far from you.
Let your *eyes* look straight ahead,
And your *eyelids* look right before you.
Ponder the path of your *feet*,
And let all your ways be established.
Do not turn to the right or the left;
Remove your *foot* from evil. (Prov. 4:20–27)

The practices of keeping the heart and protecting our ears, eyes, lips, and feet reinforce one another. Our external practices affect our internal lives, and vice versa. If we neglect our hearts, we will soon drift into outward sin. But if we fail to guard the gates to the heart, sin will soon creep through its corridors. "Set a guard on the outward senses," writes Ambrose. "The eyes must be guarded; nor is that all; take heed also of lending thy ears to filthy talking, corrupt speeches, wanton discourses, and profane songs."[9] When we fail to consider our ways, temptation clambers into our hearts through an unwatched gate. This means we cannot tend our hearts without considering the websites we visit, the books we read, the shows and movies we watch, the places we frequent, and the music and messages that fill our ears.

The discipline of watching is like a home security system. An effective surveillance system includes several components,

---

9. Isaac Ambrose, *The Christian Warrior* (London: R. B. Seely and W. Burnside, 1837), 99–100. In another treatise Ambrose writes, "That we may watch over our hearts, observe we these directions.... Guard we the windows of our souls, the senses." *Prima, Media, et Ultima*, 124.

such as security cameras, motion sensors, floodlights, electric locks, and high-decibel alarms. All these components serve one purpose: protecting the home from dangerous intruders. In similar fashion, watchfulness embraces a variety of practices, such as self-examination, prayer, meditation, and accountability, but all governed by the single intention of keeping the heart.

Guarding these gates has never been more important than it is today. We live in a media-drenched culture, a world that assaults our senses and our souls with a ceaseless barrage of sights, sounds, images, and ideas. Not all this media is overtly sinful. In God's common grace, human beings often create artistic things characterized by goodness, truth, and beauty. But we must be wary. Infernal saboteurs lurk around every digital corner. If we're not careful, Facebook will tempt us to envy and vanity, Netflix will bombard us with sensuality and triviality, and Spotify will seduce us into spiritual slumber with its constant, never-ending playlists. Eye-gate and ear-gate are under attack!

Like Job, we should make a covenant with our *eyes*, to keep our hearts from lust (Job 31:1). Like the psalmist, we should pray, "Turn away my *eyes* from looking at worthless things, and revive me in Your way" (Ps. 119:37); and "Set a guard, O LORD, over my *mouth*; keep watch over the door of my *lips*" (Ps. 141:3). The apostle John warns that we must "not love the world or the things in the world. If anyone loves the world, the love of the Father is not in him. For all that is in the world—the lust of the flesh, the lust of the *eyes*, and the pride of life—is not of the Father but is of the world" (1 John 2:15–16). And Jesus says, "Therefore take heed how you *hear*" (Luke 8:18). The only way to watch your heart is to guard the gates of your soul.

Don't Give Sin an Opportunity

"But put on the Lord Jesus Christ, and make no provision for the flesh, to fulfill its lusts" (Rom. 13:14). As we have already learned, watchfulness means wakefulness. Knowing the day of salvation is near, the apostle Paul rouses believers to cast off the works of darkness and don the armor of light (Rom. 13:12). To walk in the light of day, we must put away every sort of sinful behavior (Rom. 13:13). But we must also refuse to give sin an opportunity. That's what it means to "make no provision for the flesh." Therefore, having come to know the state and condition of your heart, "watch against all occasions and opportunities, employments, societies, retirements, businesses, as are apt to entangle thy natural temper or provoke thy corruption."[10]

Heed these wise father's instructions to his son:

> Do not enter the path of the wicked,
> And do not walk in the way of evil.
> Avoid it, do not travel on it;
> Turn away from it and pass on. (Prov. 4:14–15)

Let's make this concrete for the contemporary Christian. I've already mentioned the dangers of technology. Are you using technology to make provisions for the flesh, or have you determined to give sin no opportunity? For example, are you tempted to use pornography? Get a filter on your computer. Disable the Internet browser on your smartphone. Get an accountability partner, someone who will pray with you when you are tempted, who will hold out the gospel to you when you fail, and who will help you learn to identify and turn from

---

10. Owen, *Of Temptation*, in *Works*, 6:133.

sinful sexual desires. Are you prone to making comparisons with others, leading to feelings of unhappiness and discontent? Maybe you should abstain from social media. Whatever the temptation, watching means avoiding the occasions of sin. Owen explains, "Herein lies no small part of that wisdom which consists in our ordering our conversation aright. Seeing we have so little power over our hearts when once they meet with suitable provocations, we are to keep them asunder, as a man would do fire and the combustible parts of the house wherein he dwells."[11] Keep your heart as far from the opportunities to sin as you would keep a can of gasoline from an open flame.

Another aspect of this direction is to quickly quench the flaming arrows of temptation as soon as they come. We must never forget that these fiery darts of Satan "are prepared in the forge of his own malice."[12] His aim in temptation is always and ever to lead us into the worst evil. Like a serpent, he deceives. Like a lion, he devours. Moreover, his goal is not merely our transgressions against God's law but our loss of the gospel. As Owen observes, Satan uses sin to assault our interest in Christ.[13] This is one reason why we must deal swiftly with sin, even little sins:

> Catch us the foxes,
> The little foxes that spoil the vines,
> For our vines have tender grapes. (Song 2:15)

---

11. Owen, *Of Temptation*, in *Works*, 6:133.

12. Owen, *Of Temptation*, in *Works*, 6:95.

13. This paragraph is my paraphrase of Owen. See *Of Temptation*, in *Works*, 6:135.

Jonathan Edwards's Seventy Resolutions

The famous New England pastor Jonathan Edwards exemplified the practice of watchfulness. When he was only nineteen years of age, Edwards penned seventy resolutions for holy living. His diaries suggest that he regularly used these resolutions as a means of self-examination. One of his biographers notes that Edwards's "watchfulness over himself—over his external conduct and over his secret thoughts and purposes—was most thorough and exemplary."

He continues,

> The fear of God, and a consciousness of his own weakness, made him habitually apprehensive of sin, and led him most carefully to avoid every temptation. His self-examination was regular, universal, and in a sense constant. Every morning he endeavoured to foresee, and to guard against, the dangers of the day. Every night he carefully reviewed the conduct of his mind, during its progress, and inquired, wherein he had been negligent; what sin he had committed; wherein he had denied himself; and regularly kept an account of every thing which he found to be wrong. This record he reviewed at the close of the week, of the month, and of the year, and on the occurrence of every important change in life; that he might know his own condition, and that he might carry his sins in humble confession before God….

Every course of conduct, which led him in the least to doubt of the love of God; every action of his mind, the review of which would give him uneasiness in the hour of death, and on his final trial; he endeavoured, with all his strength, to avoid. Every obvious sin he traced back to its original, that he might afterward know where his danger lay. Every desire, which might prove the occasion of sin,—the desire of wealth, of ease, of pleasure, of influence, of fame, of popularity,—as well as every bodily appetite, he strove not only to watch against, but habitually and unceasingly to mortify; regarding occasions of great self-denial as glorious opportunities of destroying sin, and of confirm-ing himself in holiness; and uniformly finding that his greatest mortifications were succeeded by the greatest comforts.[a]

Edwards thus serves as an example of each of the first three strategies for cultivating watchfulness. He labored to know himself, taking regular inventory of his life. He exer-cised vigilance over his bodily appetites, thus guarding the gates of his senses. And he was ruthless in refusing to give opportunities to sin.

---

a. Sereno Dwight, *Memoirs of Jonathan Edwards, in The Works of Jonathan Edwards* (repr., Carlisle, Pa.: Banner of Truth Trust, 1974), 1: clxxxiv. Edwards's resolutions are readily available on many websites.

"Tiny foxes spoil the vineyards; and little sins do mischief to the tender heart," writes Spurgeon.[14]

How, then, do we face these temptations when they come? Meet them with "thoughts of faith concerning Christ on the cross," advises Owen; "this will make it sink before thee."[15] Only the shield of faith can quench the fiery darts of Satan (Eph. 6:16).[16]

Store Your Heart with the Gospel

Cultivating watchfulness involves both negative and positive disciplines: avoiding and mortifying sin on one hand, and setting our hearts on the Lord Jesus on the other. To return to the castle metaphor, we must not only guard the gates of our souls from dangerous intruders but also store our hearts with the gospel.

All persons act out of principles already in their hearts. "A good man out of the good treasure of his heart brings forth good things, and an evil man out of the evil treasure brings forth evil things" (Matt. 12:35). This, no doubt, is why the psalmist says, "Your word I have hidden in my heart, that I might not sin against You" (Ps. 119:11). The word "hidden" in this passage means to conceal, store up, or treasure something highly valued. In other words, it is only when we garrison our hearts with God's word that we can keep ourselves from sin.

---

14. C. H. Spurgeon, *Morning and Evening: A New Edition of the Classic Devotional Based on The Holy Bible, English Standard Version*, revised and updated by Alistair Begg (Wheaton, Ill.: Crossway, 2003), May 30 reading.

15. Owen, *Of Temptation*, in *Works*, 6:135.

16. For a magnificent meditation on how the shield of faith quenches the fiery darts of both "enticing" and "affrighting" temptations, see Gurnall, *Christian in Complete Armour*, 2:76–123.

As someone once quipped, "Either this Book will keep you from sin, or sin will keep you from this Book."

Imagine you lead an ancient city that will soon be besieged by a violent horde of barbarian warriors. The opposing army has marched to war. You know they are coming. There is nowhere to run, no place to hide. Your city will soon be blockaded and attacked. Your only hope for survival is to fortify the walls and store plenty of food to sustain your people when the battle comes. The more you have stockpiled, the longer you will last.

This is the picture Owen had in mind in the following direction:

> Be sure to lay in provision in store against the approaching of any temptation. This also belongs to our watchfulness over our hearts…. When an enemy draws nigh to a fort or castle to besiege and take it, oftentimes, if he find it well manned and furnished with provision for a siege, and so able to hold out, he withdraws and assaults it not. If Satan, the prince of this world, come and find our hearts fortified against his batteries, and provided to hold out, he not only departs, but, as James says, he flees….
>
> Gospel provisions will do this work; that is, keep the heart full of a sense of the love of God in Christ. This is the greatest preservative against the power of temptation in the world.[17]

By "gospel provisions," Owen means the promises of the gospel in contrast to the threats of the law, such as "fear of death, hell, punishment, with the terror of the Lord

---

17. Owen, *Of Temptation*, in *Works*, 6:133.

in them."[18] To be sure, law threats have their place. In fact, Owen says that we should also "lay in provisions of the law." But "these are far more easily conquered" than gospel provisions. Many people fear death and hell, yet are easily overcome by temptation:

> But store the heart with a sense of the love of God in Christ, with eternal design of his grace, with a taste of the blood of Christ, and his love in the shedding of it; get a relish of the privileges we have thereby: our adoption, justification, acceptance with God. Fill the heart with thoughts of the beauty of holiness, as it is designed by Christ for the end, issue, and effect of his death; and thou wilt, in an ordinary course of walking with God, have great peace and security as to the disturbance of temptations.[19]

As you can see, a watchful heart is *not* a heart preoccupied with itself, but with Christ and the great things of the gospel. If you haven't noticed yet, this is the drumbeat of this book. An Olympic runner sets his gaze on the finish line, not on his feet. In the same way, watchful Christians keep their eyes on the prize (Phil. 3:13–14).

Keep a Steadfast Focus on Christ

Introspection is one of the subtlest threats to healthy Christian spirituality. This is especially dangerous in a book focused on watchfulness. Introspection turns a person's gaze inward. Like sin itself, it can leave the soul *incurvatus in se*, curved in on itself. Introspection is myopic and parasitic; its field of

---

18. Owen, *Of Temptation*, in *Works*, 6:134.
19. Owen, *Of Temptation*, in *Works*, 6:134.

vision narrow and small. Left unchecked, introspection leaves our souls weak and anemic as it diverts our attention away from the majesty of God, the grace of Christ, and the fresh breeze of the Spirit.

The practice of watchfulness requires vigilance over ourselves, *but it must never be focused on the self.* The unswerving gaze of our souls should be forward, upward, outward, and onward. As we saw in chapter 1, expectancy is a key ingredient to watchfulness. We watch with eyes set forward as we anticipate the coming of our Lord (Matt. 24:42; 25:13; Luke 12:37; Rev. 16:15). Watching also involves an upward look, for Paul tells us to set our minds on things above, where Christ is seated at the right hand of God (Col. 3:1–2). Like marathon runners, we don't stare at our feet, but outward and onward to the finish line, indeed to Christ Himself. We run the race set before us by "looking unto Jesus, the author and finisher of our faith" (Heb. 12:2).

The greatest masters of spiritual life recognized and taught this. In one of his final books, Owen urges believers to "live in constant contemplation of the glory of Christ," believing that "when the mind is filled with thoughts of Christ and his glory, when the soul thereon cleaves unto him with intense affections, they will cast out...the causes of spiritual weakness."[20] Indeed, only this steady sight on Christ can produce true watchfulness.

Perhaps no one has helped me learn *how* to look to Christ better than the nineteenth-century Scottish pastor Robert Murray M'Cheyne. M'Cheyne once wrote a letter to someone he had never met but whose spiritual case had been made

---

20. Owen, *Glory of Christ Applied*, in *Works*, 1:460–61.

known to him. In his letter to this anonymous struggling Christian, M'Cheyne gave the advice for which he is perhaps best known. He said, "Do not take up your time so much with studying your own heart as with studying *Christ's heart*. 'For one look at yourself, take ten looks at Christ!'"[21] That's it! That's the key.

In his own earnest pursuit of Christ-centered holiness, M'Cheyne followed the advice he gave to others. This is most obvious in his "Personal Reformation," the document I mentioned in the introduction. Part of his program for reforming his personal life involved the regular practice of confessing his sins. The young preacher earnestly desired to maintain a clear conscience, "always washed in Christ's blood." This led him to plan regular times in his schedule for self-examination and confession. "I think I ought at certain times of the day—my best times,—say, after breakfast and after tea,—to confess solemnly the sins of the previous hours, and to seek their complete remission."[22]

M'Cheyne was nothing if not thorough. He resolved to confess the sins of his youth, his sins before and since conversion, his sins against light and knowledge, his sins against love and grace, and his sins against each person of the Godhead. "I ought to look at my sins" he wrote, "in the light of

---

21. Robert Murray M'Cheyne to anonymous, March 20, 1840, in Bonar, *Memoir & Remains*, 279. To another correspondent M'Cheyne said, "Learn much of the Lord Jesus. For every look at yourself, take ten looks at Christ. He is altogether lovely. Such infinite majesty, and yet such meekness and grace, and all for sinners, even the chief! Live much in the smiles of God. Bask in His beams. Feel His all-seeing eye settled on you in love, and repose in His almighty arms." Robert Murray M'Cheyne to George Shaw, September 16, 1840, in Bonar, *Memoir & Remains*, 293.

22. Bonar, *Memoir & Remains*, 150.

the holy law, in the light of God's countenance, in the light of the cross, in the light of the judgment-seat, in the light of hell, in the light of eternity."[23] He even purposed to examine his dreams; his "habits of thought, feeling, speech, and action"; the slanders of his enemies; and the bantering of his friends. M'Cheyne's regimen for self-examination was detailed, exhaustive, and systematic.

But lest you think he was overly introspective, carefully consider the healthy Christ-centeredness of the following paragraphs:

I ought to go to Christ for the forgiveness of each sin. In washing my body, I go over every spot, and wash it out. Should I be less careful in washing my soul? I ought to see the stripe that was made on the back of Jesus by each of my sins. I ought to see the infinite pang thrill through the soul of Jesus equal to an eternity of my hell for my sins, and for all of them. I ought to see that in Christ's bloodshedding there is an infinite over-payment for all my sins. Although Christ did not suffer more than infinite justice demanded, yet He could not suffer at all without laying down an infinite ransom.

I feel, when I have sinned, an immediate reluctance to go to Christ. I am ashamed to go. I feel as if it would do no good to go,—as if it were making Christ a minister of sin, to go straight from the swine-trough to the best robe,—and a thousand other excuses; but I am persuaded they are all lies, direct from hell. John argues the opposite way: "If any man sin, we have an advocate with the Father"; Jer. 3:1 and a thousand other scriptures are against it. I am sure there is neither peace nor safety from deeper sin, but in going directly to the Lord

---

23. Bonar, *Memoir & Remains*, 151.

Jesus Christ. This is God's way of peace and holiness. It is folly to the world and the beclouded heart, but it is the way.

I must never think a sin too small to need immediate application to the blood of Christ. If I put away a good conscience, concerning faith I make shipwreck. I must never think my sins too great, too aggravated, too presumptuous,—as when done on my knees, or in preaching, or by a dying bed, or during dangerous illness,—to hinder me from fleeing to Christ. The weight of my sins should act like the weight of a clock: the heavier it is, it makes it go the faster.

I must not only wash in Christ's blood, but clothe me in Christ's obedience. For every sin of omission in self, I may find a divinely perfect obedience ready for me in Christ. For every sin of commission in self, I may find not only a stripe or a wound in Christ, but also a perfect rendering of the opposite obedience in my place, so that the law is magnified, its curse more than carried, its demand more than answered.[24]

As you can see, M'Cheyne's consciousness of his sins did not obstruct his vision of Christ. Instead, his sins drove him to the Savior. This is crucial. While you and I are commanded to watch our hearts, our predominant focus must be on Christ, not ourselves. Christ is our substitute, and His atoning work more than compensates for our sins. "I ought to see the stripe that was made on the back of Jesus by each of my sins," wrote M'Cheyne. There is no malady of soul that His stripes cannot cure. No transgressions His obedience will not cover. Whatever your sins may be, whatever dark stains

---

24. Bonar, *Memoir & Remains*, 151–52.

mar your integrity this very moment, Jesus beckons you to hide yourself in His wounds.[25]

Take all your sins, the big ones and the small ones, to Jesus. Take them to the cross.

> My sin, O the bliss of this glorious thought!
> My sin, not in part, but the whole,
> Is nailed to the cross, and I bear it no more;
> Praise the Lord, praise the Lord, O my soul![26]

This is the only balm for a wounded conscience, the only hope for a sinful soul. This is the only way to deal with our hearts. You must run to Christ. And once you're there, at His feet, stay there, for your only safety is found in Him. As Jesus told His disciples, "Without Me you can do nothing" (John 15:5). The reality of our impotence apart from Christ leads directly to the next direction.

Prayerfully Depend on the Spirit

Never forget the Savior's words: "Watch *and* pray" (Matt. 26:41). Watching and praying always go together. To watch without praying is to overestimate our strength and to sin in self-reliance. To pray without watching is to disregard the Lord's command in presumptuous pride. In the words of

---

25. "Now then, we are ambassadors for Christ, as though God were pleading through us: we implore you on Christ's behalf, be reconciled to God. For He made Him who knew no sin to be sin for us, that we might become the righteousness of God in Him" (2 Cor. 5:20–21).

26. Horatio Spafford, "It Is Well with My Soul" (1873), in the public domain.

William Bridge, "Watching doth note our diligence, praying doth note our dependence."[27]

Prayer is the way we express our dependence on God. To be prayerless is to be self-sufficient. Calvin calls prayer "the chief exercise of faith."[28] Through prayer we grasp the promises of God with the hand of faith. To be prayerless, then, is to be faithless, unbelieving. Prayerlessness is practical atheism. "Prayer," writes William Gurnall, "is the channel in which the stream of divine grace, blessing, and comfort runs from God the fountain into the cistern of their hearts."[29] When we neglect prayer, we dam up this channel of grace and comfort. Prayerlessness leaves us in a spiritual drought.

Moreover, to be prayerless is to be careless and to fail in our watch. In Owen's words, "He that would be little in temptation, let him be much in prayer."

> This calls in the suitable help and succor that is laid up in Christ for us (Heb. 4:16). This casteth our souls into a frame of opposition to every temptation.... The soul so framed is in a sure posture.... If we do not abide in prayer, we shall abide in cursed temptations. Let this, then, be another direction: Abide in prayer, and that expressly to this purpose, that we "enter not into temptation." Let this be one part of our daily contending with God, that he would preserve our souls, and keep our hearts and our ways, that we be not entangled... that he would give us diligence, carefulness, and watchfulness over our own ways.[30]

---

27. William Bridge, "A Lifting Up for the Downcast" (sermon 8), in *The Works of the Rev. William Bridge*, M. A. (London: Thomas Tegg, 1845), 2:153.

28. Calvin, *Institutes*, 3.20 (800).

29. Gurnall, *Christian in Complete Armour*, 2:500.

30. Owen, *Of Temptation*, in *Works*, 6:126–27.

Prayer thus brings both objective and subjective benefits. Prayer lays hold of God's help for us through Christ our Great High Priest. And prayer changes the disposition of our hearts, producing within us a humble, watchful frame of heart. When we pray, we declare our inherent weakness and our dependence on God.

Pray especially for God to strengthen and fill you by His Spirit (Eph. 3:16; 5:18). The Holy Spirit is the author of our regeneration, the agent of our sanctification, the illuminator of biblical truth, and the Helper who leads us into the things of Christ (Titus 3:5; 2 Thess. 2:13; Eph. 1:17–18; John 14:26, respectively).

In Bunyan's *Holy War*, after Emmanuel returns to Mansoul and gives the city a new charter, he appoints as Lord Chief Secretary "a person of no less quality and dignity than is my Father and I." This secretary will be Mansoul's "chief teacher; for it is he, and he only, that can teach you clearly in all high and supernatural things.... Nor can any, as he, tell Mansoul how and what they shall do to keep themselves in the love of my Father. He also it is that can bring lost things to your remembrance, and that can tell you things to come."[31] The secretary, of course, is the Holy Spirit.

No amount of trying to watch will safeguard our lives if we lack the sustaining, preserving influence of God's Spirit. That's why Jude says, "Praying in the Holy Spirit, keep yourselves in the love of God" (Jude 20–21). The manner or means by which we keep ourselves in God's love is by praying in the Holy Spirit.

And while it is true that no Christian can be utterly without the Spirit (Rom. 8:9), we also know that the Spirit can

---

31. Bunyan, *Holy War*, 163–64.

be both grieved and quenched (Eph. 4:30; 1 Thess. 5:19). We must, therefore, not only watch but also pray for the continuing work of the Spirit in our hearts and lives.

M'Cheyne, once more, provides a good example. The second part of his "Personal Reformation" concerned his desire to be "filled with the Holy Spirit at all times." This led him to meditate on his weakness apart from Christ and the constant need for prayer. "To be filled with the Holy Spirit, I am persuaded that I ought to study more my own weakness," he wrote.

> I ought to pray and labour for the deepest sense of my utter weakness and helplessness that ever a sinner was brought to feel. I am helpless in respect of every lust that ever was, or ever will be, in the human heart. I am a worm—a beast—before God. I often tremble to think that this is true. I feel as if it would not be safe for me to renounce all indwelling strength, as if it would be dangerous for me to feel (what is the truth) that there is nothing in me keeping me back from the grossest and vilest sin. This is a delusion of the devil. My only safety is to know, feel, and confess my helplessness, that I may hang upon the arm of Omnipotence.[32]

But as with his practice of confession, M'Cheyne's study of his weakness did not terminate on himself but on the sufficiency of Christ and the Spirit. Notice how he directs his focus to Christ in the following excerpts:

> I ought to study Christ as a living Saviour more,—as a Shepherd, carrying the sheep He finds,—as a King, reigning in and over the souls He has redeemed,—as a Captain, fighting with those who fight with me,

---

32. Bonar, *Memoir & Remains*, 153.

Ps. 35,—as one who has engaged to bring me through all temptations and trials, however impossible to flesh and blood.

I am often tempted to say, How can this Man save us? How can Christ in heaven deliver me from lusts which I feel raging in me, and nets I feel enclosing me? This is the father of lies again! "He is able to save unto the uttermost."

I ought to study Christ as an Intercessor. He prayed most for Peter, who was to be most tempted. I am on his breastplate. If I could hear Christ praying for me in the next room, I would not fear a million of enemies. Yet the distance makes no difference; He is praying for me....

I ought to study the Comforter more,—his Godhead, his love, his almightiness. I have found by experience that nothing sanctifies me so much as meditating on the Comforter, as John 14:16.[33]

M'Cheyne's journals demonstrate the earnest, humble, thoroughly Christ-centered prayerful watch we so desperately need: diligence wed to dependence; and a growing awareness of personal weakness joined with bold, prayerful confidence in the Savior's all-sufficient strength, made ours through the gift of His Holy Spirit.

Cherish the Grace You Have Received

A garden needs to be not only weeded but also watered. This horticultural principle holds true in our spiritual lives as well. Just as sin must be mortified—that is, crucified and killed (Rom. 8:13; Gal. 5:24; Col. 3:5)—so grace must be vivified, or cherished and strengthened. According to Owen, "The

---

33. Bonar, *Memoir & Remains*, 154.

main of our spiritual watch and diligence consisteth in the cherishing, improving, and increasing of the grace that we have received, the strengthening of the new creature that is wrought in us."[34]

Scripture teaches this in many ways. Consider the "put off" and "put on" language so common in Paul's letters. The rags of sin, like old and worn clothing, are to be cast aside. In their place, we are to put on the garments of righteousness (Rom. 13:12–14; Eph. 4:22–24; Col. 3:8–14). We find further examples in the metaphors of growing physically (Eph. 4:11–16; 1 Peter 2:1–3), building a temple (Eph. 2:19–22; 1 Peter 2:4–5), and bearing fruit (Gal. 5:22–23; Phil. 1:9–11; Col. 1:9–10). These pictures each emphasize different aspects of growth in grace. And the many commands to "grow" and "abound" in the graces of faith, hope, and love show that growth is to be not only prayerfully sought but diligently pursued. This is just the basic biblical teaching on sanctification.

Owen's point is that watchfulness consists in nourishing the grace we have received so as to further the growth. By "cherishing, improving, and increasing" the graces wrought within us by God's Spirit, we not only survive but thrive. For as M'Cheyne said, "I am persuaded that nothing is thriving in my soul unless it is growing."[35]

Bunyan creatively establishes this point in The Holy War. When Emmanuel retakes Mansoul, he installs numerous captains in the city to help govern and guard it from future attacks. These noble captains include five soldiers named

---

34. Owen, Psalm CXXX, in Works, 6:592.
35. Bonar, Memoir & Remains, 156.

Credence, Good-hope, Charity, Innocent, and Patience[36]—
each captain clearly representing a unique Christian grace.
But it is Emmanuel's charge to the city concerning his captains that is especially helpful. Mansoul is urged to treat them
well, indeed to "love them, nourish them, succour them."

> If therefore any of them should, at any time, be sick
> or weak, and so not able to perform that office of love
> which with all their hearts they are willing to do—
> and will do also when well and in health—slight them
> not, nor despise them, but rather strengthen them, and
> encourage them, though weak and ready to die (Heb.
> 12:12); for they are your fence, and your guard, your wall,
> your gates, your locks, and your bars. And although,
> when they are weak, they can do but little, but rather
> need to be helped by you, than that you should then
> expect great things from them, yet when well, you know
> what exploits, what feats and warlike achievements they
> are able to do, and will perform for you.
>
> Besides, if they be weak, the town of Mansoul can-
> not be strong; if they be strong, then Mansoul cannot
> be weak; your safety therefore doth lie in their health,
> and in your countenancing of them (Isa. 35:3). Remem-
> ber also that if they be sick, they catch that disease of
> the town of Mansoul itself (Rev. 3:2; 1 Thess. 5:14).[37]

The defense and safety of our souls are closely tied to the
health and strength of our graces. That is why growing in
grace is a means to watchfulness.

---

36. Bunyan, *Holy War*, 86. The captains' standard-bearers are also
noteworthy. Mr. Promise is the standard-bearer for Captain Credence, Mr.
Expectation for Captain Good-hope, Mr. Pitiful for Captain Charity, Mr.
Harmless for Captain Innocent, and Mr. Suffer-long for Captain Patience.

37. Bunyan, *Holy War*, 166–67.

Boston's Three Dimensions of Watching

Thomas Boston was a Scottish pastor and theologian who lived near the end of the Puritan era. In his sermon "Christian Watchfulness Stated, and Enforced," Boston says there are some things we must watch over, some things we must watch against, and some things we must watch for. Boston's headings provide a helpful three-dimensional praxis for the practice of watchfulness.

I. There are some things we must watch over to keep them right.

   1. Watch over yourselves.
      Watch over your heads, your principles.
      Watch over your hearts.
      The thoughts of the heart must be watched.
      Watch also over the affections of the heart.
      Watch over your tongues.
      Your senses must also be watched.
      Watch over your feet, your walk and conversation.

   2. Watch over your graces.

   3. Watch over your duties.

   4. Watch over your attainments.

II. There are some things we must watch against.

   1. Watch against your lusts and corruptions.

Watch against the sin of your nature.

Watch against your former sins.

Watch against your particular sins, to which you find yourselves inclined.

Watch against little sins.

2. Watch against appearances of evil.

3. Watch against occasions of sin.

4. Watch against temptations to sin.

5. Watch against evil company.

III. There are some things we must watch for, as men watching for advantages against the enemy, and for strengthening themselves.

1. Watch for the proper season of duty.

2. Watch for the motions of the Spirit.

3. Watch for experiences, by observing carefully the dispensations of providence towards you.

4. Watch the success of your duties.[a]

---

a. Thomas Boston, "Christian Watchfulness Stated, and Enforced," in *The Whole Works of Thomas Boston*, ed. Samuel M'Millen (Aberdeen: George and Robert King, St. Nicholas Street, 1848), 4:387–94.

Persevere in the Word of Christ

In his treatise on temptation, Owen's last general direction for watching comes from Revelation 3:10 (KJV): "Because thou hast kept the word of my patience, I also will keep thee from the hour of temptation, which shall come upon all the world, to try them that dwell upon the earth." Owen takes the phrase "word of my patience" as a subjective genitive, thus describing the patience of Christ toward His saints. Perhaps a better way to view this is as an attributive genitive, thus describing Christ's word about patience (that is, perseverance). Nevertheless, Owen's exposition is both theologically rich and pastorally helpful.

Owen says that three things are implied in keeping this word: we must know the word with the mind, cherish the word in the heart, and obey the word from the will.[38] We must know the word with the mind in all its dimensions. As a word of grace and mercy, it saves us; as a word of holiness and purity, it sanctifies us; as a word of liberty and power, it sets us free; and as a word of consolation, it comforts and supports us in every condition of life.[39] But we must also treasure the word because of its great value. As Paul says, we must "guard the good deposit" of the gospel (2 Tim. 1:14, ESV) and hold fast the faithful word we have been taught (Titus 1:9). This will lead to obedience.[40]

---

38. Or to use Owen's terms, keeping the word of Christ's patience involves knowledge, valuation, and obedience. Owen, *Of Temptation*, in *Works*, 6:139.

39. Owen, *Of Temptation*, in *Works*, 6:139–40.

40. "He that, having a due acquaintance with the gospel in its excellencies, as to him a word of mercy, holiness, liberty, and consolation, values it, in all its concernments, as his choicest and only treasure,—makes it his business and the work of his life to give himself up unto it in universal obedience,

Owen then discusses several reasons why believers who keep this word will be preserved from temptation. For one thing, this is a promise that Christ will preserve His people, and every promise is sealed by "the *faithfulness* of the Father ...the *grace* of the Son...and the *power* and *efficacy* of the Holy Ghost."[41] In other words, this promise is backed and guaranteed by an eternal, threefold, covenant bond. Our perseverance in obedience is thus ensured by God's preserving grace: "Where the promise is, there is all this assistance. The faithfulness of the Father, the grace of the Son, the power of the Spirit, are all engaged in our preservation."[42]

Keeping the word also works subjectively on our hearts by keeping us in a watchful, spiritual disposition. By mortifying our hearts to the world, we are made less susceptible to temptation. "He that keeps close to Christ is crucified with him," writes Owen, "and is dead to all the desires of the flesh and the world [Gal. 6:14]."[43] But more than that, "in this frame the heart is *filled with better things*,"[44] and this also fortifies us against temptation.

Finally, perseverance in Christ's word furnishes us with "preserving considerations and preserving principles."[45] These considerations include thoughts of Christ and His glory; Christ's conquest over temptations as our brother, captain,

---

then especially when opposition and apostasy put the patience of Christ to the utmost,—he shall be preserved from the hour of temptation." Owen, *Of Temptation*, in *Works*, 6:141.

41. Owen, *Of Temptation*, in *Works*, 6:141–42.

42. Owen, *Of Temptation*, in *Works*, 6:142.

43. Owen, *Of Temptation*, in *Works*, 6:143.

44. Owen, *Of Temptation*, in *Works*, 6:143. Emphasis original.

45. Owen, *Of Temptation*, in *Works*, 6:143.

and king; and the fear of losing fellowship with Him. The preserving principles are the Spirit-wrought graces of faith, which empties the soul of its own wisdom and engages the heart of Christ for assistance; and love, especially love for the saints, which animates our hearts with care for others.[46]

But note this: the key to maintaining this disposition, these considerations, and these principles is a holy preoccupation with the magnificence of Christ Himself. Only when we are ravished in communion with Christ will we be liberated from lesser loves:

> When the soul is exercised to communion with Christ, and to walking with him, he drinks new wine, and cannot desire the old things of the world, for he says, "the new is better." He tastes every day how gracious the Lord is; and therefore longs not after the sweetness of forbidden things,—which indeed have none. He that makes it his business to eat daily of the tree of life will have no appetite unto other fruit…. This the spouse makes the means of her preservation; even the excellency which, by daily communion, she found in Christ and his graces above all other desirable things. Let a soul exercise itself to a communion with Christ in the good things of the gospel,—pardon of sin, fruits of holiness, hope of glory, peace with God, joy in the Holy Ghost, dominion over sin,—and he shall have a mighty preservative against all temptations. As the full soul loathes the honey-comb,—as a soul filled with carnal, earthly, sensual pleasures finds no relish nor savor in the sweetest spiritual things; so he that is satisfied with the kindness of God…has a holy contempt of the

---

46. Owen, *Of Temptation*, in *Works*, 6:145–47.

baits and allurements that lie in prevailing temptatio
and is safe.[47]

Once again we see that communion with Christ is the key to
watchfulness. The directions we've studied in this chapter are
all aimed at this target. Let's turn to one more practice that
can help us preserve this watchful frame of heart.

Develop a Daily Rhythm for Walking with God

From Old Testament to New, the Scriptures describe godly
living in terms of walking with God (cf. Gen. 5:24; 6:9; 17:1;
Rev. 3:4). In the ancient world, walking was the primary mode
of travel. Most ordinary people couldn't afford camels or
horses, and it would be several millennia before bicycles (not
to mention planes, trains, and automobiles) were invented. So
they walked. Walking thus served as a vivid metaphor for the
believer's pilgrimage.

But a journey of any distance is made up of steps. You
cannot walk from one village to the next without taking steps
on a road from here to there. And the same is true of walking with God. Our progress from the City of Destruction to
the Celestial City encompasses thousands of individual steps.
That's why learning to walk with God daily is so important. If
you want to keep a close watch on your heart, you need to get
a rhythm for walking with God.

The Reformers and Puritans gave much attention to this.
They were concerned not only with the reformation of doctrine but of practical daily life. With this end in view, they
wrote voluminously about the daily routines and rhythms of

---

47. Owen, *Of Temptation*, in *Works*, 6:144. I've slightly edited this quotation by updating archaic words with modern equivalents.

the Christian life. Calvin, for example, prescribes set times
throughout the day for prayer: "When we arise in the morning, before we begin daily work, when we sit down to a meal,
when by God's blessing we have eaten, when we are getting
ready to retire." The Reformer no doubt recognized the biblical injunction to pray always. "We should ever aspire to God
and pray without ceasing," he writes; "still, since our weakness
is such that it has to be supported by many aids, and our sluggishness such that it needs to be goaded, it is fitting each one
of us should set apart certain hours for this exercise."[48]

In their pastoral discourses and books, the English Puritans went even further in recommending detailed regimens
for ordering the daily lives of Christians. For example, the
fourth of Rogers's *Seven Treatises* is taken up with "directing
the believer unto a daily practice of a Christian life."[49] Rogers
describes the "necessary parts of the daily direction" in terms
of eight specific biblical priorities:

48. Calvin, *Institutes*, 3.20.50 (917–18). As Boulton (quoting Herman Sel-
derhuis) notes, "This cycle amounts to 'virtually a monastic rule.'" Matthew
Myer Boulton, *Life in God: John Calvin, Practical Formation, and the Future of
Protestant Theology* (Grand Rapids: Eerdmans, 2011), 39. In many ways, Calvin
was critical of the monastic system and wary of encouraging "any superstitious
observance of hours, whereby, as if paying our debt to God, we imagine ourselves paid up for the remaining hours." He rather viewed this program for
daily prayer as "a tutelage for our weakness, which should be thus exercised
and repeatedly stimulated." *Institutes*, 3.20.50. For more on how Calvin adapted
and democratized monastic practices for instructing the piety of ordinary
believers, see Boulton, *Life in God*. For examples of the kinds of prayers Calvin
prescribed, see John Calvin, *Tracts and Letters* (Edinburgh: Banner of Truth
Trust, 2009), 2:95–99.
49. Rogers, *Seven Treatises*, 319.

1. First, that every day we should be humbled for our sins, as through due examination of our lives by the law of God we shall see them.

2. That every day we be raised up in assured hope of the forgiveness of them, by the promises of God in Christ.

3. That every day we prepare our hearts "to seek the Lord" still, and keep them fit and willing thereto.

4. That every day we strongly and resolutely arm ourselves against all evil and sin, fearing most of all to offend God.

5. That every day we nourish our fear and love of Him, and joy in Him more than in any thing, and endeavor to please Him in all duties, as occasion shall be offered, "looking for His coming" (2 Thessalonians 3:5).

6. That every day our thanks be continued for benefits received, and still certainly hoped for.

7. That every day "we watch and pray" for steadfastness and constancy in all these.

8. That every day we hold and keep our peace with God, and so lie down with it.[50]

Then, to maintain these biblical priorities, Rogers prescribed nine daily practices. These duties encompassed every

---

50. Rogers, *Seven Treatises*, 341–42.

aspect of daily life, although Rogers clarified that these duties were "most commonly to be done daily, but not of necessity."

The first duty, of awaking with God.

The second duty, of beginning the day with prayer.

The third duty, about our callings.

The fourth rule or duty, directing us in company.

The fifth duty, how we should behave ourselves in solitariness [solitude].

The sixth duty, of using prosperity well.

The seventh duty, of bearing afflictions rightly every day they come.

The eighth duty, namely, of using religious exercises in our families.

The ninth and last duty, of viewing the day.[51]

Many other Puritans followed suit, including Lewis Bayly, who published *The Practice of Piety: Directing a Christian How to Walk, that He May Please God* in 1611, and Henry Scudder, who wrote *The Christian's Daily Walk in Holy Security and Peace* in 1631, a book that made a strong impression on John Owen in his youth.

A casual first glance at these works could turn off twenty-first-century believers. Even in his own day, Richard Rogers was once accosted by the lord of a local manor who asked why he was so precise. Rogers replied, "O sir, I serve a precise God."[52]

---

51. Rogers, *Seven Treatises*, 359–63.
52. J. I. Packer, *A Quest for Godliness: The Puritan Vision of the Christian Life*, ministry ed. (Wheaton, Ill.: Crossway, 2012), 114.

To be sure, sometimes the Puritans prescribed rules that went beyond direct scriptural authority. Yet attentive readers will observe that they were constant in directing believers to place their trust in Christ and His righteousness, not in the performance of duties. Furthermore, most of the duties they recommended were nothing more than concrete applications of general biblical commands. As Rogers explains:

> Yet let none think, that I mean to set down to them particularly what actions they shall do every day, for they are for the most part variable and innumerable (on the six days especially) and therefore impossible to be enjoined; but only such as bind the conscience every day, and cannot without sin be omitted: and yet such, as are neither too many to be learned to the troubling of the memory; nor so few, but that they yield great furtherance to the true Christian for the well passing of the day. *This daily direction then of a Christian, is a gathering together of certain rules out of God's word, by which we may be enabled every day to live according to the will of God*, with sound peace: and therefore the following of such direction is a faithful and constant endeavor to please God in all things every day, as long as we live here to the peace of our conscience, and to the glorifying of him.[53]

So the aim of recommending a daily routine isn't to saddle you with burdensome extrabiblical duties but to help you embrace a practical daily rhythm of life that keeps you rooted in God's word, trusting in Christ's grace, and relying on the Spirit's power.

---

53. Rogers, *Seven Treatises*, 339. Emphasis added.

This is precisely what M'Cheyne was striving after in his "Personal Reformation." In the second part of this document, which he called "Reformation in Secret Prayer," M'Cheyne wrote down resolutions for his prayer life. Here is a sampling:

> I ought to pray before seeing any one. Often when I sleep long, or meet with others early, and then have family prayer, and breakfast, and forenoon callers, often it is eleven or twelve o'clock before I begin secret prayer. This is a wretched system. It is unscriptural.... I can do no good to those who come to seek from me. The conscience feels guilty, the soul unfed, the lamp not trimmed. Then, when secret prayer comes, the soul is often out of tune. I feel it is far better to begin with God—to see His face first—to get my soul near to Him before it is near another.... In general, it is best to have at least one hour alone with God, before engaging in anything else.... I am persuaded that I ought never to do anything without prayer, and, if possible, special, secret prayer.... I ought to spend the best hours of the day in communion with God. It is my noblest and most fruitful employment.... I ought not to give up the good old habit of prayer before going to bed.... I ought to read three chapters of the Bible in secret every day, at least.[54]

When I read these words, I feel a mixture of conviction, inspiration, and holy envy. I am convicted of my sins of neglect. But I am also inspired by M'Cheyne's example of godliness and feel a holy envy of his nearness to Jesus. The details of my life are different from M'Cheyne's: he was a young, single pastor in the bustling, industrial city of Dundee in nineteenth-century Scotland; I am a middle-aged, married

---

54. Bonar, *Memoir & Remains*, 156–58.

father of four in twenty-first-century America, with all the complexities of modern life. So my routines will not look the same. But I pray that God will grant me such a heart.

Your daily rhythm will depend in large part on your station in life. The schedules of a single college student and a mother of preschoolers will be quite different. But every believer should heed the apostolic command: "But you, beloved, *building* yourselves up on your most holy faith, *praying* in the Holy Spirit, keep yourselves in the love of God, *looking* for the mercy of our Lord Jesus Christ unto eternal life" (Jude 20–21). Every day we all should be building, praying, and looking. As you cultivate the discipline of watchfulness, make this prayer from Augustus Toplady your own:

> Ah! Give me, Lord, myself to see,
> Against myself to watch and pray,
> How weak am I, when left by thee,
> How frail, how apt to fall away!
> If but a moment thou withdraw,
> That moment sees me break thy law.
>
> Jesus, the sinner's only trust,
> Let me now feel thy grace infus'd!
> Ah! raise a captive from the dust,
> Nor break a reed already bruis'd!
> Visit me, Lord, in peace again,
> Nor let me seek thy face in vain.[55]

---

55. Augustus Toplady, Poem 19, in *The Works of Augustus Toplady* (Harrisburg, Va.: Sprinkle Publications, 1997), 889–90.

Examine and Apply

1. Set aside some time for taking inventory of your life. What are your specific weaknesses and temptations? What are your "Delilah sins"? Pray Psalm 139:23–24:

   > Search me, O God, and know my heart;
   > Try me, and know my anxieties;
   > And see if there is any wicked way in me,
   > And lead me in the way everlasting.

2. Think through the "gates" to your heart and soul. Which gates do you need to guard more carefully? Assess your use of all forms of media: computer, television, smartphone, Internet, and social media. Are there specific activities or habits that you need to change in order to better watch your heart? Where have you given opportunity to sin?

3. Owen says we need to store our hearts with the gospel before we come under the siege of temptation. Discuss this with a friend. What are four or five practical ways you could start storing your heart with gospel truth?

4. Read "M'Cheyne's Personal Reformation" in full (see appendix 1). How does his example of watchfulness affect you? Consider writing something similar for yourself.

5. According to Owen, "He that keeps close to Christ is crucified with him and is dead to all the desires of the flesh and the world." How close are you to Christ right now? How could you become closer?

6. Do you have a daily rhythm for walking with God? How might developing such a rhythm be helpful?

Chapter 4

When?
The Seasons for Watchfulness

And this is the first thing in our watching, to consider
well the seasons wherein temptation usually makes its
approaches to the soul, and be armed against them.

—John Owen, *Of Temptation: The Nature and Power
of It; the Danger of Entering Into It; and
the Means of Preventing that Danger*

Great airplane pilots, military generals, and football coaches
share at least one thing in common: they have prepared for
worst-case scenarios and are trained to make strategic deci-
sions under pressure. The Christian life requires similar
forethought. Urging his followers to count the cost of disciple-
ship, Jesus compares them to a man gauging the expense of
his building project and a king's careful considerations before
waging war (Luke 14:27–33). Paul instructed Christians to
prepare for battle by remembering their enemies and arming
themselves with the full armor of God (Eph. 6:10–18). Such
preparation is essential for those who wish to "withstand in
the evil day" (Eph. 6:13).

The purpose of this chapter, then, is to provide some
scenario-based training. John Owen says that "the first thing
in our watching" is "to consider well the seasons wherein

temptation usually makes its approaches to the soul, and be armed against them."[1] While Owen considers four such seasons, his fellow Puritan John Flavel names twelve.[2] With help from Owen, Flavel, and others, we will consider seven.

Watching in Seasons of Prosperity

One of these is "a season of unusual outward prosperity." Owen warns that "prosperity and temptation go together; yea, prosperity is a temptation, many temptations, and that because, without eminent supplies of grace, it is apt to cast a soul into a frame and temper exposed to any temptation."[3]

The biblical support for this warning is vast. In the book of Proverbs, we read that "the turning away of the simple shall slay them, and the prosperity of fools shall destroy them" (Prov. 1:32, KJV). Prosperity often takes the edge off our moral and spiritual senses. If created goods are not "received with thanksgiving" and "sanctified by the word of God and prayer" (1 Tim. 4:4–5), they easily become idols, seductive substitutes that draw us away from the Lord.

As Agur prayed,

> Remove falsehood and lies far from me;
> Give me neither poverty nor riches—
> Feed me with the food allotted to me;
> Lest I be full and deny You,
> And say, "Who is the LORD?"
> Or lest I be poor and steal,
> And profane the name of my God. (Prov. 30:8–9)

---

1. Owen, *Of Temptation*, in *Works*, 6:131.

2. Flavel, *Saint Indeed*, in *Works*, 5:417–509.

3. Owen, *Of Temptation*, in *Works*, 6:127.

"There is a hardness, an insensible want of spiritual sense, gathered in prosperity, that, if not watched against, will expose the heart to the deceits of sin and baits of Satan," writes Owen.[4] This echoes Paul's warnings to Timothy:

> Now godliness with contentment is great gain. For we brought nothing into this world, and it is certain we can carry nothing out. And having food and clothing, with these we shall be content. But those who desire to be rich fall into temptation and a snare, and into many foolish and harmful lusts which drown men in destruction and perdition. For the love of money is a root of all kinds of evil, for which some have strayed from the faith in their greediness, and pierced themselves through with many sorrows. (1 Tim. 6:6–10)

Once more, I find helpful an illustration from *The Holy War*. After Emmanuel reclaims Mansoul, their enemy Diabolus is enraged and calls a council of war, made up of "all the princes of the pit," including old Incredulity, Apollyon, Beelzebub, and Lucifer. Their purpose is to devise a plan for retaking the castle. The strategy they concoct is genius. With the help of Mr. Sweet-world and Mr. Present-good, "men that are civil and cunning, but our true friends and helpers," the demonic horde contrive a plot for luring Mansoul from their watch. Here is an excerpt from Lucifer's speech:

> Let Mansoul be taken up in much business, and let them grow full and rich, and this is the way to get ground of them. Remember ye not that thus we prevailed upon Laodicea, and how many at present do we hold in this snare? Now, when they begin to grow full,

---

4. Owen, *Of Temptation*, in *Works*, 6:128.

they will forget their misery, and if we shall not affright them, they may happen to fall asleep and so be got to neglect their town-watch, their castle-watch, as well as their watch at the gates.

Yea, may we not, by this means, so cumber Mansoul with abundance that they shall be forced to make of their castle a warehouse instead of a garrison fortified against us and a receptacle for men of war?

This plan is met with applause by Diabolus's war council and is "accounted the very masterpiece of hell, to wit, to choke Mansoul with a fullness of this world, and to surfeit her heart with the good things thereof."[5]

This is not to deny, however, that material prosperity is one of God's many earthly gifts. Scripture speaks not only about the dangers of wealth but also of its benefits and blessings. We do well to obey Ecclesiastes 7:14 ("In the day of prosperity be joyful") while also remembering that "cares, riches, and pleasures of life" can choke the word (Luke 8:14).

The real issue, as a well-worn yet still helpful cliché puts it, is not what you possess but what possesses you. Earthly blessings, held loosely in the grateful hands of faith and used in appropriate measure, are a means of doing good to family, friends, and neighbors. But we must guard our hearts with vigilance in seasons of prosperity, lest we "fall into temptation and a snare, and into many foolish and harmful lusts which drown men in destruction and perdition" (1 Tim. 6:9).

---

5. Bunyan, *Holy War*, 247–50.

Watching in Times of Solitude

What do you do when you're alone? What do you think, feel, daydream about, and desire? What do you read, watch, and listen to? Do you tend your soul and guard your heart in solitude?

Owen observed that time spent alone can be either your best time or your worst. Times of solitude can be rich seasons of prayer, meditation, and fellowship with God, or they can be occasions of temptation and sin. We need to be watchful in times of solitude:

> We must watch over our times of solitude and retirement, by night or by day, more carefully than any other time. In these times we see what we are—these are either the best or the worst of our times, when the predominant principle in us will show itself.[6]

Solitude reveals who you really are. Times of solitude are an index to the heart. You may wear a religious mask at church. Maybe you paste on a smile at work or school. But your inward thoughts and desires show your true face. As someone once said, "What a man is on his knees before God, that he is, and nothing more."[7]

---

6. John Owen, *Gospel Evidences of Saving Faith* (Grand Rapids: Reformation Heritage Books, 2016), 100. This is a modernized edition edited by Brian G. Hedges. For the original, see Owen, *Gospel Grounds and Evidences of Saving Faith*, in *Works*, 5:455.

7. This statement is often attributed to M'Cheyne, but I have not found it in any of his writings. John Owen, on the other hand, did say something similar. In describing how indwelling sin "works *by negligence of private communion with God in prayer and meditation*," Owen said, "Indeed, what men are *in these duties* (I mean as to faith and love in them), that they are, and no more." And again, "What a man is in secret, in these private duties, that he is in the eyes of God, and no more." Owen, *Indwelling Sin*, in *Works*, 6:300. Owen makes a similar statement in *Gospel Grounds and Evidences of Saving Faith*: "There are

But times of solitude can also be times of great temptation. In a letter to a friend, M'Cheyne once confessed, "I feel
the assaults of Satan most when I am removed into a corner;
every evil thought and purpose rushes over my soul, and it is
only at times that I can find Him whom my soul loveth."[8]

We see this pattern also in Scripture. David was tempted
when alone on the rooftop while Jesus was tempted in the
solitude of the garden. The problem, of course, is not solitude.
In fact, the problem is not temptation. Both David and Jesus
were tempted in solitude, but David succumbed while Jesus
resisted. The problem is the failure to watch. This is the reason why Owen recommends "a firm watchfulness over times
of solitude both night and day, with a continual readiness to
fight temptations at their first appearance in order that they
will not surprise the soul."[9]

The need for vigilance in solitude is more urgent today
than ever. So many sins are committed in solitude. Smart-
phones provide constant access to the Internet and media.
Pornography is only a few clicks away. Even if you avoid more
overt forms of evil, there is always the pull of the latest news.
I am not saying all these things are necessarily sinful. But the
proliferation of social media, games, and apps has brought into
our lives a ceaseless and unprecedented potential for diversion
and distraction. We need to watch both *what* forms of media
we ingest and *how* we ingest them. We need to both consider

---

none to be so diligently watched over as our solitudes and retirements by night
or by day. What we are in them, that we are indeed, and no more." Owen,
Gospel Grounds, in *Works*, 5:455.

8. Robert Murray M'Cheyne to Rev. R. MacDonald, January 12, 1839, in
Bonar, *Memoir & Remains*, 210.

9. Owen, *Gospel Evidences*, 100. See also *Gospel Grounds*, in *Works*, 5:455.

the content we consume and count the minutes and hours we spend consuming it.

On the other hand, so much growth can happen in solitude. You can pray. You can read, memorize, and meditate on God's word. You can listen to Christ-exalting sermons and worshipful music. There are dozens of ways for you to feed your soul in private. So please do not hear me saying that you should avoid solitude. God has given us both public and private means of grace. Neither should be neglected.

We do not need to avoid solitude. But we do need to remain watchful so that we use our times of solitude in ways that honor Christ and nourish our own souls. "The great design, in the exercise of this grace," writes Owen, "is to keep and preserve the soul constantly in an humble and contrite frame; if that be lost at any time, the whole design is for that season disappointed."[10]

One of the main differences between true believers and false professors is seen in how they use their solitude. This is another one of Owen's observations: "As to the performance of duties, and so the enjoyment of outward privileges, fruitless professors often walk hand in hand with them; but now come to their secret retirements, and what a difference is there! There the saints hold communion with God: hypocrites, for the most part, with the world and their own lusts."[11]

As an illustration, consider how the quality of a marriage is reflected in how a given couple spends their time alone together. When a husband and wife genuinely love each other, they will prefer their spouse to all other company. Nothing will

---

10. Owen, *Gospel Evidences*, 100.
11. Owen, *Of Communion*, in *Works*, 2:38–39.

Flavel's Seasons for Keeping the Heart

John Flavel's *A Saint Indeed* is a book-length exposition and application of Proverbs 4:23 (KJV): "Keep thy heart with all diligence; for out of it are the issues of life." Often reprinted as *Keeping the Heart*, Flavel's treatise outlines twelve seasons in which the heart must be watched and kept. While only some of those seasons are discussed in this chapter, here is Flavel's full list.

1. The time of prosperity, when providence smiles upon us.

2. The time of adversity, when providence frowns upon us.

3. The time of Zion's troubles, when the church is oppressed.

4. The time of danger and public distraction.

5. The time of straits and outward pinching wants.

6. The season of duty, when we draw nigh to God in public, private, or secret duties.

7. When we receive injuries and abuses from men.

8. When we meet with great cross and provocations.

9. The hour of temptation, when Satan lays close siege to the fort-royal of the Christian's heart.

10. The time of doubting and spiritual darkness.

11. When sufferings for religion come to an height.

12. The time of sickness, when a child of God draws nigh to eternity.

Flavel not only elaborates on each one of these headings but he also provides an astonishing arsenal of means, motives, arguments, and helps for keeping the heart in these various seasons, which, taken together, amount to all of life!

Flavel also urges the great necessity of this duty for the glory of God, the sincerity of our profession, the beauty of our conversation (or conduct), the comfort of our souls, the improvement of our graces, and the stability of our souls in the hour of temptation.[a]

---

a. John Flavel, *A Saint Indeed (or, The Great Work of a Christian Opened and Pressed)*, in *The Works of John Flavel* (1820; repr., Edinburgh: Banner of Truth Trust, 1968).

delight them more than their shared moments of friendship, intimacy, and affection. A troubled marriage, however, will be the opposite. While the unhappy couple may put on a public façade of love, their private moments will be marked by cool civility, bitter strife, or distant aloofness from one another as they each bury themselves in activities that exclude the other. Similar dynamics are true in our spiritual marriage to Christ. Whatever we pretend in public, the truth of our relationship with Him is evident in how we treat Him in solitude.

Watching When Grace Is in Slumber

We should also watch in "a time of the slumber of grace" (or "spiritual drowsiness"), "of neglect in communion with God."[12] These are those times when our lamps burn dim and our zeal grows cold, when we've grown negligent in spiritual disciplines and have left our first love. "If thou art drowsing in such a condition as this, take heed," warns Owen. "Thou art falling into some woeful temptation that will break all thy bones, and give thee wounds that shall stick by thee all the days of thy life."[13]

Owen also describes this as a time "of formality in duty."[14] I take this to mean that the spiritually drowsy believer is still going through religious motions, even though his heart has begun to wander. He reads Scripture, mouths prayers, and attends worship, but does so with little faith, hope, or love. He draws near to the Lord with his lips, but his heart is far from God. Gurnall also warns against spiritual drowsiness and

---

12. Owen, *Of Temptation*, in *Works*, 6:128.
13. Owen, *Of Temptation*, in *Works*, 6:129.
14. Owen, *Of Temptation*, in *Works*, 6:128.

points out three dangerous symptoms of it: (1) "an unwilling-ness and backwardness to duty," (2) "formality in prayer," and (3) "prevalency of wandering thoughts."[15]

To illustrate this dangerous condition, both Gurnall and Owen refer to the spouse who lost the company of her beloved in Song of Songs 5:2–8:[16]

> I sleep, but my heart is awake;
> It is the voice of my beloved!
> He knocks, saying,
> "Open for me, my sister, my love,
> My dove, my perfect one;
> For my head is covered with dew,
> My locks with the drops of the night."
> I have taken off my robe;
> How can I put it on again?
> I have washed my feet;
> How can I defile them?
> My beloved put his hand
> By the latch of the door,
> And my heart yearned for him.
> I arose to open for my beloved,
> And my hands dripped with myrrh,
> My fingers with liquid myrrh,
> On the handles of the lock.
> I opened for my beloved,
> But my beloved had turned away and was gone.
> My heart leaped up when he spoke.
> I sought him, but I could not find him;
> I called him, but he gave me no answer.

---

15. Gurnall, *Christian in Complete Armour*, 2:505.

16. Gurnall, *Christian in Complete Armour*, 2:505; Owen, *Of Temptation*, in *Works*, 6:128.

The watchmen who went about the city found me.
They struck me, they wounded me;
The keepers of the walls
Took my veil away from me.
I charge you, O daughters of Jerusalem,
If you find my beloved,
That you tell him I am lovesick!

This passage describes a common difficulty experienced by partners in marriage: a growing distance in the relationship. In this passage, it is one-sided. The husband comes seeking his bride, but she is too comfortable, too sluggish, to put effort into the relationship. He doesn't cajole or chide, but he does withdraw. And then, when her heart begins to yearn for him, she opens the door—but too late! He is absent, nowhere to be found. She goes into the streets to search for her beloved but is assaulted and abused by the city guards. This leaves her miserable, lonely, and lovesick.[17]

This spiritual reading of the Song of Songs reminds us that the deep intimacy and love we crave is found only in communion with God. As Augustine of Hippo wrote in his *Confessions*, "You made us for yourself, and our hearts find no peace till they rest in you."[18] But in our sloth and sluggishness, we sometimes neglect the calls of our Beloved and consequently lose the delight of fellowship with Him.

---

17. "She slept," Owen observes, "and was drowsy, and unwilling to gird herself to a vigorous performance of duties, in a way of quick, active communion with Christ. Before she is aware, she hath lost her Beloved; and then she moans, inquires, cries, endures woundings, reproaches, and all, before she obtains him again." Owen, *Of Temptation*, in *Works*, 6:128.

18. Saint Augustine, *Confessions*, trans. R. S. Pine-Coffin (New York: Penguin Books, 1961), 21 (1.1).

Haven't you found the bride's experience to be true in your relationship with Christ? Haven't there been times when you sought Him but found Him not? And haven't there been times when He has come to you, when you knew the sweet invitation of His voice, when the Spirit of your Lord called, beckoning you to fellowship with Him, and yet you failed to heed His call? Do these words of William Cowper echo your own experience?

> Where is the blessedness I knew,
> When first I saw the Lord?
> Where is the soul refreshing view
> Of Jesus and His Word?
>
> What peaceful hours I once enjoyed!
> How sweet their memory still!
> But they have left an aching void
> The world can never fill.[19]

The only way to prevent further backsliding and sin in this condition is to watch and pray. As the Lord Jesus said to the church of Sardis, "Be watchful, and strengthen the things which remain, that are ready to die" (Rev. 3:2). "If any that reads the word of this direction be in this condition," writes Owen, "let him now awake, before he is entangled beyond recovery. Take this warning from God; despise it not."[20]

Watching in Seasons of Self-Confidence

Renewing our watch in seasons of spiritual slumber seems obvious. But we must also be watchful in those seasons when

---

19. William Cowper, "O for a Closer Walk with God" (1772), in the public domain.

20. Owen, *Of Temptation*, in *Works*, 6:129.

we feel good about our spiritual lives. Have you been faithful in your daily devotions? Has it been weeks, or even months, since you last blew it with anger or lust? Are you starting to feel like a pretty good Christian? Watch out! The enemy of your soul lies in wait. As Paul exhorts, "Let him who thinks he stands take heed lest he fall" (1 Cor. 10:12).

Do you remember the story of Peter on the night before the crucifixion? Jesus warned His disciples that they would all fall away and one would betray Him (Matt. 26:20–21, 30–31). But Peter protested his superior loyalty to Jesus: "Lord, I am ready to go with You, both to prison and to death," he said (Luke 22:33). Peter viewed himself as the most faithful of all the disciples. Though they might all fall away, he would not (Matt. 26:33).

But we know the story. True to Jesus's words, Peter denied Jesus three times by morning. After the third denial, Luke tells us that "the Lord turned and looked at Peter. Then Peter remembered the word of the Lord, how He had said to him, 'Before the rooster crows, you will deny Me three times.' So Peter went out and wept bitterly" (Luke 22:61–62).

Only after Peter's courage collapsed into a heap of denials and oaths did Peter truly begin to see his weakness, depravity, and sin. As Owen observes, "This taught him so far to know himself all his days."[21] Through his failure, Peter learned the danger of placing confidence in himself. Perhaps this is the reason he later urged his fellow believers to pass the time of their pilgrimage in fear (1 Peter 1:17) and to watch in vigilance for their adversary, the devil (1 Peter 5:8).

_____

21. Owen, *Of Temptation*, in *Works*, 6:130.

When we read this story, we should put ourselves in Peter's place and realize that our virtues aren't as virtuous as we suppose them to be. When we think we're at our best, there are cracks beneath the surface, flaws that Jesus sees, and weaknesses that could lead us to deny our Lord.

Do you realize that given the right circumstances, sufficient temptation, and enough pressure, you are capable of committing the worst sins imaginable? Has God begun to unveil your heart to you? The more self-confidence you have, the more precarious your position. But the more of your weakness you see, the better you are prepared to watch and pray with confidence, not in yourself but in God:

> Let the heart, then, commune with itself and say, "I am poor and weak; *Satan* is subtle, cunning, powerful, watching constantly for advantages against my soul; the *world* earnest, pressing, and full of specious pleas, innumerable pretenses, and ways of deceit; my *own corruption* violent and tumultuous, enticing, entangling, conceiving sin, and warring in me, against me; *occasions* and advantages of temptation innumerable in all things I have done or suffer, in all businesses and persons with whom I converse; the *first beginnings* of temptation insensible and plausible, so that, left unto myself, I shall not know that I am ensnared, until my bonds be made strong, and sin hath got ground in my heart: therefore on God alone will I rely for preservation, and continually will I look up to him on that account."[22]

---

22. Owen, *Of Temptation*, in *Works*, 6:125. Italics original. I've slightly edited this quotation by updating archaic words with modern equivalents.

"Seven Abominations in My Heart"

In his spiritual autobiography, *Grace Abounding to the Chief of Sinners*, John Bunyan confessed.

I find to this day seven abominations in my heart:

1. Inclining to unbelief;

2. Suddenly to forget the love and mercy that Christ manifesteth;

3. A leaning to the works of the law;

4. Wanderings and coldness in prayer;

5. To forget to watch for that I pray for;

6. Apt to murmur because I have no more, and yet ready to abuse what I have;

7. I can do none of those things which God commands me, but my corruptions will thrust in themselves. When I would do good, evil is present with me.

Though he lamented these sins, Bunyan also believed God in His wisdom ordered them for his good, encouraging him to greater humility and watchfulness and deeper dependence on Christ:

1. They make me abhor myself;

2. They keep me from trusting my heart;

3. They convince me of the insufficiency of all inherent righteousness;

4. They show me the necessity of flying to Jesus;

5. They press me to pray unto God;

6. They show me the need I have to watch and be sober;

7. And provoke me to pray unto God, through Christ, to help me, and carry me through this world.[a]

---

a. John Bunyan, *Grace Abounding to the Chief of Sinners*, in *The Whole Works of John Bunyan*, ed. George Offor (London: Blackie and Son, Paternoster Row, 1862), 1:50.

You are absolutely helpless. The enemy will attack. Temptation will come. But left to yourself, you are like a tumbleweed in a tornado, a handkerchief in a hurricane. The lion will roar, the viper will strike, the flaming arrows of temptation will fly, and you will fall—*apart from grace*. That is why you need God. Beware of self-confidence.

Watching in Seasons of Doubt and Discouragement

We must also be watchful in seasons of doubt, when our faith is weak. The Christian life, we must remember, is "the good fight of *faith*" (1 Tim. 6:12). Though we are believers, the relics of unbelief still slink through our hearts like sleeper agents, ready to ambush us in an instant. The war against unbelief is a daily one (Heb. 3:12–13), but we also face seasons when the assault on our faith is more intense.

Sometimes this comes in the wake of adversity, when we are tempted to doubt God's faithfulness rather than trust His promises. The psalmists often experienced this and cried, "How long, O LORD?" (cf. Psalms 13, 80, and 94). But even in their laments, they engaged in prayer, "the chief exercise of faith."[23] Our problems start not when we face adversity or express lament, but when we cease to take our anxieties to God in prayerful faith.

Unbelief is, in fact, the taproot of all other sins. The enemy of our souls remembers this, even when we do not. That's why he keeps our faith in his crosshairs. "*Unbelief* is the primary cause of all our inquietude, from the moment that our hearts are drawn to seek salvation by Jesus," writes John Newton.

---

23. Calvin, *Institutes*, 3.20 (800).

This inability to take God at his word, should not be merely lamented as an infirmity, but watched, and prayed, and fought against as a great sin. A great sin indeed it is; the very root of our apostasy, from which every other sin proceeds. It often deceives us under the guise of humility, as though it would be presumption, in such sinners as we are, to believe the declarations of the God of truth. Many serious people, who are burdened with a sense of other sins, leave this radical evil out of the list. They rather indulge it, and think they ought not to believe, till they can find a warrant from marks and evidences within themselves.[24]

But like the Hydra in Greek mythology, unbelief has many heads. Sometimes it swaggers as cool cynicism while other times it whimpers in self-pity. One of its darkest faces is discouragement, which sometimes leads to despair.

Do you remember when Giant Despair locks Christian and Hopeful in Doubting Castle? Bunyan describes it as a "very dark dungeon" that was "nasty and stinking to the spirit of these two men." There they lay in darkness for four days, "without one bit of bread, or drop of drink, or Light, or any to ask how they did," such that Christian feels "double sorrow." The giant beats them mercilessly with his cudgel, taunting them "to make an end of themselves, either with Knife, Halter or Poison: For why, said he, should you choose Life, seeing it is attended with so much Bitterness?"

But don't forget how they escape! Christian remembers that he has a key in his pocket called Promise. And with that key, the two beleaguered saints unlock every door and unbolt

24. John Newton, "Thoughts on Faith and the Assurance of Faith," in *The Works of John Newton* (Edinburgh: Banner of Truth Trust, 1988), 6:468.

every gate in the dungeon, until they finally find their way to freedom.[25]

Watching during the Interruptions of Routine

We also need vigilance during seasons of interruption to our normal routines. These interruptions include the welcome respites of vacation, travel, and visits with friends and loved ones, as well as the less-wanted intrusions of sickness, adversity, and loss. But whether positive or negative, all such disruptions carry the potential to knock us off balance—to blow us off course in our devotional lives and expose us to unique, unusual, and unexpected temptation.

Have you ever experienced this? Maybe you've been on a regular Bible-reading plan and have enjoyed daily times of prayer and meditation for weeks or months on end. And then a holiday comes and with it a house full of guests. First you just skimp on Bible reading. But before you know it, you've altogether quit praying in private. Only after several days of drift and an angry blowup with your spouse do you realize what has happened.

Bunyan illustrates this temptation in the story of the arbor placed halfway up Hill Difficulty. Though the arbor was "made by the Lord of the hill for the refreshing of weary travelers," Christian lapses into a fateful sleep in which he loses his roll (that is, his assurance). Only when he later meets Timorous and Mistrust does the pilgrim realize his error. With many tears, he retraces his steps until he recovers his roll, all the while "bewailing his sinful sleep, saying, O wretched Man that I am! That I should sleep in the Day-time! That I should sleep

---

25. Bunyan, *Pilgrim's Progress*, 128–35.

in the midst of Difficulty! That I should so indulge the Flesh, as to use that rest, for ease to my flesh, which the Lord of the Hill hath erected only for the relief of the Spirits of Pilgrims!"[26]

Christian's error was not in the *use* of rest, but in its *abuse*. And this is a trap many believers face, especially during time off, when we welcome the break from many normal responsibilities. But if we extend our vacation to our spiritual lives, we will soon be in trouble. As Martyn Lloyd-Jones said, "There is no such thing as a holiday in the spiritual realm."[27]

The sequel to Christian's experience in the arbor, recorded in part 2 of *The Pilgrim's Progress*, is also instructive. Like her husband before her, Christiana also takes her rest in the arbor. And like him, she also suffers loss when she forgets "to take her bottle of spirits with her." Her companion Mercy thus observes: "I think this is a losing place. Here Christian lost his Roll; and here Christiana left her bottle behind her; Sir, what is the Cause of this?" Their guide, Mr. Great-heart, answers: "The cause is Sleep, or Forgetfulness; some sleep when they should keep awake, and some forget when they should remember; and this is the very cause, why often at resting places, some Pilgrims, in some things, come off losers. Pilgrims should watch, and remember what they have already received under their greatest enjoyments; but for want of doing so, oft-times their rejoicing ends in tears, and their sun-shine in a Cloud."[28] So whether you find yourself climbing Hill Difficulty or resting in the arbor, beware of dropping your guard.

---

26. Bunyan, *Pilgrim's Progress*, 43.

27. D. Martyn Lloyd-Jones, *Preaching and Preachers* (Grand Rapids: Zondervan, 1972), 165.

28. Bunyan, *Pilgrim's Progress*, 255–56.

Watching in the Moment of Temptation

Finally, how do you watch in the moment of temptation itself? I'm not talking about the fleeting, seemingly benign thought of sin that may hold initial allure but is easily dismissed, though we should be on guard against these kinds of thoughts too.

No, I'm talking about that moment when you've savored the juicy morsel and like the taste. You clamp down your jaws and suddenly feel the sharp, piercing desire for more and a forceful tug toward deliberate, willful sin. You realize that you've swallowed a hook and the angler is reeling you in. Your better judgment, God's word, and the Holy Spirit are whispering "no." But your appetites and emotions are screaming "yes!"

I have in mind those times when you are like Peter in the courtyard, your heart frenzied by fear, about to commit an act of cowardice and treachery; or David on the rooftop, seized by lust's hot desire, teetering on the brink of adultery; or Moses at the rock, boiling in anger, poised to open a valve that will erupt into a rebellious torrent of volcanic rage. Can you still escape temptation when you're in *that* deep?

Owen certainly thought so and provided not only analysis and diagnosis for tempted souls, with directions for watching and praying to avoid temptation, but also offered counsel to the person already in temptation's tenacious grip: "Suppose the soul has been surprised by temptation, and entangled at unawares, so that now it is too late to resist the first entrances of it. What shall such a soul do that it be not plunged into it, and carried away with the power thereof?"[29] Owen counsels four things that are both helpful and hopeful.

---

29. Owen, *Of Temptation*, in *Works*, 6:131.

First, pray. Ask the Lord for help. You're about to sink under the waves. The water is up to your neck. You are gasping for air but gulping mouthfuls of water. Your breath is gone. You are about to go under. What do you do? Owen advises, "Do as Paul did: beseech God again and again that it may 'depart from thee' (2 Cor. 12:8)."[30] Cry out with Peter, "Lord, save me!" Jesus will stretch out His hand and catch you (Matt. 14:30–31). This is the first and most immediate step. Pray. Stop and do it now.

Second, run to Jesus. Run to Jesus, who has already conquered temptation as your representative, in your place.[31] Running to Jesus is, of course, what we do when we pray. But when you are strongly tempted, don't just turn to Jesus in general. Run to Him for specific, tangible help, remembering that He has already conquered temptation in your place: "For in that He Himself has suffered, being tempted, He is able to aid those who are tempted.... For we do not have a High Priest who cannot sympathize with our weaknesses, but was in all points tempted as we are, yet without sin. Let us therefore come boldly to the throne of grace, that we may obtain mercy and find grace to help in time of need (Heb. 2:18; 4:15–16). Remember this: Jesus was tempted first and foremost not as our example but as our brother, captain, and king. Adam, our first representative, was tempted in Paradise and failed. Jesus, the second Adam and our final representative, was tempted in the desert and conquered. As our hero and champion, Christ

---

30. Owen, *Of Temptation*, in *Works*, 6:136.

31. "Fly to Christ, in a peculiar manner, as he was tempted, and beg of him to give thee succour in this 'needful time of trouble.'" Owen, *Of Temptation*, in *Works*, 6:136.

has already defeated and beheaded Goliath. He has crushed
the serpent's head. The battle is already won. So run, weary
Christian. Run to your conquering King!

Then, third, expect the Lord to deliver you. This is His
promise[32]: "No temptation has overtaken you except such as is
common to man; but God is faithful, who will not allow you
to be tempted beyond what you are able, but with the temptation will also make the way of escape, that you may be able to
bear it" (1 Cor. 10:13). Expect Him to fulfill it.

And keep in mind that the Lord has many ways of deliv-
ering you.[33] He may send an affliction or a trial that takes
the edge off your appetite for sin and restores your hunger for
His word. "Before I was afflicted I went astray, but now I keep
Your word" (Ps. 119:67). He may give you sufficient grace to
endure the temptation (2 Cor. 12:8–9; James 1:12). He may
rebuke the enemy, so that he flees from you (Zech. 3:1–2;
James 4:7). Or He may revive you with some refreshing comfort from His Spirit and encouragement from His word. But
be sure of this: the Lord has more ways to deliver than Satan
has ways to tempt. "Greater is he that is in you, than he that
is in the world" (1 John 4:4, KJV).

Finally, after you've found some immediate relief from
the Lord, repair the breach[34] and get back on the happy, narrow road of righteousness. I don't mean to imply that it is a
sin to be tempted. Temptations to sin and sinful acts are not
the same things. But sometimes (not always) when we are
tempted, it is our fault. Sometimes we are tempted because

---

32. Owen, *Of Temptation*, in *Works*, 6:136.
33. Owen, *Of Temptation*, in *Works*, 6:137.
34. Owen, *Of Temptation*, in *Works*, 6:137.

we have ventured too far from God or too close to the arena of temptation. "Watch and pray that you may not enter into temptation" implies that watchfulness and prayerfulness can prevent temptation and that temptation will be the inevitable consequence of failing to watch and pray. To neglect watching and praying, then, is also a sin.

Therefore, it is important to figure out why and how we entered into temptation in the first place. Big sins always follow little sins. Sins of commission usually follow sins of omission, sins of neglect. So when you have found yourself unusually tempted, follow the trail back. Ask the Lord to search you and know your heart, to try you and know your thoughts, to see if there is any grievous way in you and to lead you in the way everlasting (Ps. 139:23–24). You will probably find carelessness, prayerlessness, and negligence.

But even here, in your repentance, you must not only turn *from* temptation and sin but also turn *to* Christ. He is the one who both preserves the tempted and restores the fallen (Luke 22:31–32; John 21). So wherever you are in respect to temptation and sin, seek Christ.

Examine and Apply

1. Consider the various seasons covered in this chapter. Are you in one or more of these seasons right now? Which one(s)?

2. Read Song of Songs 5:2–8 again. Describe a time when you have neglected fellowship with the Lord Jesus. What was the result? How did you recover? William Gurnall describes three symptoms of spiritual drowsiness (see page 119). Do you manifest any of these symptoms?

3. What are one or two sins you've never been tempted to commit? Has your sense of immunity from these temptations resulted in dangerous self-confidence?

4. How do you spend time when you're alone? Owen says our times in solitude "are either the best or the worst of our times." What do your practices reveal about your heart? Where is change needed?

5. How do you handle interruptions to your normal life? Do they blow you off course from regular Bible reading and prayer? How might you need to prepare differently for your next vacation?

6. What is your most common, recurrent temptation? Think through the last time you failed to resist. How did you handle the moment of temptation? Ask the Lord for grace to handle it differently next time and be quick to pray when it comes.

Chapter 5

Who?
Watchfulness in the Church

The Lord Christ hath ordained, that the members of the
same church or society should mutually watch over one
another, and the whole body over all the members, unto
their edification.... That the practice of it is so much
lost...is the shame and almost ruin of Christianity.

—John Owen, *An Exposition of the
Epistle to the Hebrews*

The Pilgrim's Progress introduces us to two characters named
Watchful. The first is the porter of Palace Beautiful, a lodge
on Christian's way to the Celestial City, "built by the Lord
of the Hill...for the relief and security of Pilgrims." This
lodge serves as a needed way station for rest and renewal in
Christian's journey after his climb up Hill Difficulty. In Christian's
approach to the porter's lodge, he faces two ferocious
lions that leave him shaking in his boots. He is tempted to
draw back in fear, but Watchful, seeing Christian halt, beckons
him forward, assuring him that the lions are chained and
that he will not be harmed if he walks in the middle of the
path. Christian heeds Watchful's advice, passes by the lions
unscathed, and finds relief in Palace Beautiful, where he is

examined, encouraged, and armed for battle by four damsels named Discretion, Prudence, Piety, and Charity.[1]

The second character named Watchful is one of the four shepherds encountered by Christian and Hopeful when they come to the Delectable Mountains.[2] The shepherds guide the pilgrims into the mountains, where they are shown the steep precipice of Mount Error, along with the unburied corpses of heretics at its base. After this they are taken to Mount Caution. The shepherds bid them look far in the distance, and they see blind men stumbling upon the tombs, unable to escape. Next, the travelers gaze through a mountainside door, where they see smoke and darkness, hear the rumbling noise of fire, and smell the acrid scent of brimstone. As the shepherds explain, this is a byway to hell, where hypocrites forsake their pilgrimage for one reason or another. Then the shepherds take Christian and Hopeful up to the high peak of Mount Clear. There they gaze through a perspective-glass (or telescope) to catch a glimpse of the Celestial City. Finally, the shepherds warn them to beware of the flatterer and to take heed not to sleep on the Enchanted Ground. Then they bid them Godspeed as the pilgrims continue their journey.

In each of these episodes, Bunyan underscores the vital role of pastors in exercising watchfulness over believers in the church. Like the porter, pastors should encourage believers

1. See Bunyan, *Pilgrim's Progress*, 45–58. As Bunyan himself commented on this scene: "How beautiful must that church be where Watchful is the porter; where Discretion admits the members; where Prudence takes the oversight; where Piety conducts the worship; and where Charity endears the members one to another!" See *Pilgrim's Progress*, in *Works*, 3:109n3.

2. Bunyan, *Pilgrim's Progress*, 137. The other three shepherds are named Knowledge, Experience, and Sincere.

to stand strong against fear and show them the safe path of holiness. Like the shepherds, pastors should help believers spot error, exercise caution, and keep their gaze set on eternal things. And throughout *The Pilgrim's Progress*, we learn that believers are not meant to walk alone. After all, where would Christian have been without the guidance of Evangelist, the example of Faithful, and the companionship of Hopeful?

In other words, watchfulness is a community project. This final chapter is thus devoted to watchfulness in the church. First, we will study the biblical teaching on pastoral watchfulness, that is, the role of elders and pastors in watching over the flock. Then, we will consider the duty of mutual watchfulness, along with several ways of putting it into practice.

Pastoral Watchfulness

Pastors and elders are especially tasked with watching over others. This is evident when we consider the metaphors often used for spiritual leaders. For example, there are at least three word pictures implicit in Paul's address to the elders of Ephesus, recorded in Acts 20:25–31:

> And indeed, now I know that you all, among whom I have gone preaching the kingdom of God, will see my face no more. Therefore I testify to you this day that I am innocent of the blood of all men. For I have not shunned to declare to you the whole counsel of God. Therefore take heed to yourselves and to all the flock, among which the Holy Spirit has made you overseers, to shepherd the church of God which He purchased with His own blood. For I know this, that after my departure savage wolves will come in among you, not sparing the flock. Also from among yourselves men will rise up, speaking perverse things, to draw away the disciples

after themselves. Therefore watch, and remember that
for three years I did not cease to warn everyone night
and day with tears.

Most obvious is the word *overseers* (*episkopos*) in verse
28. In the Greco-Roman world, the word *overseer* (sometimes
translated "bishop") was used of a guardian charged with
the "definite function or fixed office of guardianship within
a group."[3] This term and its cognates are commonly used in
the New Testament to describe spiritual leaders entrusted
with guarding and watching over God's people (see Phil. 1:1;
1 Tim. 3:1–2; Titus 1:7; 1 Peter 5:2).

This passage also employs *shepherd* imagery as Paul
exhorts the elders to "take heed to…all the flock" and "to
shepherd the church of God." As shepherds watch over sheep,
so elders are to watch over the flock of God. The task of shepherding is comprehensive; it involves leading and feeding,
watching and warning. Pastors, therefore, are not only to provide spiritual leadership and feed the flock with the nourishing
truth of God's word but also to watch over their souls and caution them against the predatory threats of false teachers. Peter
also combines the images of overseer and shepherd in 1 Peter
5:2–4, when he exhorts fellow elders to "shepherd the flock of
God which is among you, serving as overseers, not by com-
pulsion but willingly, not for dishonest gain but eagerly; nor as
being lords over those entrusted to you, but being examples
to the flock; and when the Chief Shepherd appears, you will
receive the crown of glory that does not fade away."

Paul also suggests an image more dominant in the Old Testament, *the watchman*, when he claims that having faithfully

---

3. Ardnt, Danker, and Bauer, *Greek-English Lexicon*, 379.

proclaimed the kingdom (Acts 20:25) and declared the whole counsel of God (v. 27), he is therefore "innocent of the blood of all men" (v. 26). These words allude to Ezekiel 3:16–21, where the prophet is charged with warning the house of Israel of God's judgment, much as a watchman was charged with keeping sentry over a city and warning the sleeping people of imminent dangers and threats.[4] This image soberly underscores a leader's accountability to God for the souls of those entrusted to his charge.

Hebrews 13:17 teaches the same thing, this time addressing church members rather than church leaders: "Obey those who rule over you, and be submissive, for they watch out for your souls, as those who must give account. Let them do so with joy and not with grief, for that would be unprofitable for you." Together these passages show the basis, accountability, and proper motivation for pastoral watchfulness.

---

4. In Ezekiel 3:16–21, the word of the Lord comes to Ezekiel, saying,

Son of man, I have made you a watchman for the house of Israel; therefore hear a word from My mouth, and give them warning from Me: When I say to the wicked, "You shall surely die," and you give him no warning, nor speak to warn the wicked from his wicked way, to save his life, that same wicked man shall die in his iniquity; but his blood I will require at your hand. Yet, if you warn the wicked, and he does not turn from his wickedness, nor from his wicked way, he shall die in his iniquity; but you have delivered your soul.

Again, when a righteous man turns from his righteousness and commits iniquity, and I lay a stumbling block before him, he shall die; because you did not give him warning, he shall die in his sin, and his righteousness which he has done shall not be remembered; but his blood I will require at your hand. Nevertheless if you warn the righteous man that the righteous should not sin, and he does not sin, he shall surely live because he took warning; also you will have delivered your soul.

The basis for pastoral watchfulness is the Holy Spirit's appointment of elders as overseers of God's precious flock, obtained by Christ's blood-shedding death. The church is God's dearly beloved people, whose redemption He has purchased at great cost to Himself. Church leaders must never forget this.

We've already seen one reference to accountability with the image of the watchmen. But this is explicitly emphasized in Hebrews 13:17: "for they watch out for your souls, as *those who must give account*." Shepherds are undershepherds, accountable to Christ Himself, the "Chief Shepherd" (1 Peter 5:4) of the sheep. Remember that when the Lord Jesus restored Peter after his threefold denial, He said, "Feed My sheep" (John 21:17). The sheep are His. The church does not belong to the pastor; it belongs to Christ. He loved the church enough to die for it. Pastors watch over the souls of Christ's people on His behalf and will give an account to Him.

A pastor's motivation for watching over the souls of others is not to be guilt or fear; it is to be joy. As Hebrews 13:17 points out, pastors are to watch out for the flock's souls "with joy and not with grief, for that would be unprofitable for you." Pastoral watchfulness must be driven by the joy shepherds have in helping believers find their joy in Christ. This was the constant drumbeat of Paul's ministry: "Not that we have dominion over your faith, but are fellow workers *for your joy*; for by faith you stand" (2 Cor. 1:24). "Therefore, my beloved and longed-for brethren, *my joy and crown*, so stand fast in the Lord, beloved" (Phil. 4:1). "For what is our hope, *or joy, or crown of rejoicing*? Is it not even you in the presence of our Lord Jesus Christ at His coming? *For you are our glory and joy*" (1 Thess. 2:19–20).

As church members, we can help make the ministry of pastors and elders a joy by willingly submitting ourselves to their watchful care. In fact, this is one of the reasons behind the command in Hebrews 13:17: "Obey those who rule over you, and be submissive, *for* they watch out for your souls, as those who must give account. Let them do so with joy and not with grief, for that would be unprofitable for you." Believers will most benefit from the ministry of their spiritual leaders when their relationship is characterized by loving submission to their ministry of the word.

This is not, of course, a license for the abuse or misuse of pastoral authority. The authority of pastors and elders is the ministerial authority of the word. Church members are obligated to follow their godly example and submit to their biblical teaching. But the authority of elders is subordinate to the authority of Christ and is limited by the parameters of Scripture. While elders are shepherds of the flock, they are undershepherds to Christ and servants of His word.

John Owen draws attention to the apostolic examples of pastoral care in both Galatians and Hebrews. In both cases, the church was in spiritual danger of being seduced from the simplicity of the gospel.[5] The apostle "understood their temptations and saw their dangers," Owen writes. "And with what wisdom, variety of arguments, expostulations, and awakening reproofs, doth he deal with them! what care, tenderness, compassion, and love, do appear in them all! In nothing did the excellency of his spirit more evidence itself, than in his jealousy concerning and tender care for them in such a condition."[6]

---

5. Owen, *Hebrews*, in *Works*, 20:19.
6. Owen, *Hebrews*, in *Works*, 20:19.

We also see this in 2 Corinthians 11:2–3: "For I am jealous for you with godly jealousy. For I have betrothed you to one husband, that I may present you as a chaste virgin to Christ. But I fear, lest somehow, as the serpent deceived Eve by his craftiness, so your minds may be corrupted from the simplicity that is in Christ." These words give us yet another image, as Paul pictures himself as *the father of the bride* who has betrothed the church to her husband, the Lord Jesus; but now the bride is vulnerable to being seduced away from her divine lover. So he writes and preaches to the church. He pleads with them to recognize their danger. He urges, exhorts, and warns them to remain faithful to Christ.

This is pastoral watchfulness. This is an example for all ministers—all pastors, elders, shepherds, and care group leaders. "In this care and watchfulness lie the very life and soul of their ministry," writes Owen. "Where this is wanting, whatever else be done, there is but the carcass, the shadow of it."[7] And it is a reminder to all believers that we need the local church, with its God-ordained ministry of the word.

Mutual Watchfulness

But watchfulness is not only the responsibility of elders and overseers; it is also the mutual responsibility of church members to one another. In Gurnall's words, "Every private saint hath a charge to be his brother's keeper."[8]

This fraternal duty is clear in Scripture. The apostle Paul says, "Brethren, if a man is overtaken in any trespass, you who are spiritual restore such a one in a spirit of gentleness,

---

7. Owen, *Hebrews*, in *Works*, 20:19.
8. Gurnall, *Christian in Complete Armour*, 2:510.

considering yourself [or, 'keep watch on yourself,' ESV] lest you also be tempted. Bear one another's burdens, and so fulfill the law of Christ" (Gal. 6:1–2). Notice how carefully Paul frames this exhortation. He does not give us leave to confront brothers and sisters over every trifling disagreement or concern. We are rather to confront when someone "is overtaken in any trespass." We are not to confront harshly, "but in a spirit of gentleness." Nor should we rush into correcting a fellow believer without first "considering [our]selves, lest [we] also be tempted." As Jesus taught in the Sermon on the Mount, I must remove the plank from my own eye before pointing out the speck in my brother's eye. Next, notice that the stated purpose in this exhortation is not confrontation but restoration: "restore such a one." The goal is constructive and positive, not destructive and negative.

The key to obeying this command is found in the words "you who are spiritual." When read in the context of Paul's earlier teaching in this letter, "spiritual" must refer to true believers who have received "the promise of the Spirit through faith" (Gal. 3:14) and to whom God has "sent forth the Spirit of His Son into [our] hearts, crying out, 'Abba, Father!'" (Gal. 4:6) and have been "born according to the Spirit" (Gal. 4:29). Furthermore, "you who are spiritual" refers to those who "walk in the Spirit" (Gal. 5:16) and thus produce not "the works of the flesh" (Gal. 5:19) but the "fruit of the Spirit…love, joy, peace, longsuffering, kindness, goodness, faithfulness, gentleness, self-control" (Gal. 5:22–23). As the immediately preceding verses state, "If we live in the Spirit, let us also walk in the Spirit. Let us not become conceited, provoking one another, envying one another" (Gal. 5:25–26). This passage, then, does not give license to the carnal, flesh-driven censuring of other believers so common in strife-ridden churches. It is rather a call to mature, Spirit-led, caring concern for one another in the context of brotherly love.

As a young man, I spent several years traveling on an itinerant ministry team before entering pastoral ministry. One of my regular responsibilities was to pray during worship services in a designated prayer room. I was zealous to pray but grew indignant when other team members scheduled to pray with me didn't consistently show up. And I told them so! But while I could see the speck in the eyes of others, a telephone pole was protruding from mine. My self-righteousness and anger were so out of hand that one of our team leaders pulled me from prayer ministry, confronted my pride, and asked me to sit under the ministry of the word, where the Spirit began to deal with my sinful heart.[9]

While the passage in Galatians establishes the appropriate context and tone for mutual watchfulness, Hebrews addresses the same issue with a deep sense of urgency: "Beware, brethren, lest there be in any of you an evil heart of unbelief in departing from the living God; but exhort one another daily, while it is called 'Today,' lest any of you be hardened through the deceitfulness of sin" (Heb. 3:12–13). This passage shows us why watching over one another is so necessary: the danger of being hardened in heart through the deceitfulness of sin and unbelief.[10]

John Owen also addresses the need for mutual watchfulness in the church. In a sermon titled "The Mutual Care

---

9. The brother who confronted me then is now a pastor and one of my best friends.

10. See also the discussion of this passage above in chapter 2.

of Believers over One Another," Owen defines "the church watch" as "the work of every member, according to its measure, to the increase of grace in itself and others, according to the principle of love."[11] This watch, Owen teaches, is based on our union with one another in love. Appealing to 1 Corinthians 12, Owen reminds believers that they are members of the same body and so should "have the same spiritual care of every other member as the members of the natural body have."[12]

The purpose of this watch is threefold: "the temporal, and spiritual, and eternal good of all believers." By temporal good, Owen has in mind meeting the needs of the poor. By spiritual good, he says we are to "keep up this watch" in two ways: "by the prevention of evil, on the one hand; and by recovery from evil, promotion of grace, and confirming in it, on the other hand."[13] This we should pursue through both personal example and mutual exhortation.

The problem is that we often lack three things in attending to mutual watchfulness and exhortation: love, ability, and "holy consciousness to ourselves of unbelief."[14] We will never be effective in watching over one another as long as we lack genuine love for one another, biblically informed relationship skills ("ability"), and watchfulness over our own hearts. "Nothing can conquer these things but the grace of God," Owen reminds us, "and unless we have these things, we

---

11. Owen, "The Mutual Care of Believers over One Another," in *Works*, 16:477–78.

12. Owen, "Mutual Care," in *Works*, 16:478.

13. Owen, "Mutual Care," in *Works*, 16:479.

14. Owen, "Mutual Care," in *Works*, 16:479.

cannot do it. Our recovery from any of these evils is a great part of this watch."[15]

How, then, do we go about watching over one another? What kinds of practices will help us carry out mutual watchfulness? Let's consider three: conversation, admonition, and consideration.

Conversation

By conversation I mean talking to one another. As Paul says in Ephesians 4:15, the body of Christ grows in maturity by "speaking the truth in love." In fact, many of the "one another" commands in Scripture involve the words we speak to other believers. "Let the word of Christ dwell in you richly in all wisdom, *teaching* and *admonishing* one another in psalms and hymns and spiritual songs, *singing* with grace in your hearts to the Lord" (Col. 3:16). "*Exhort* one another daily" (Heb. 3:13). "*Confess* your trespasses to one another, and *pray* for one another" (James 5:16). "*Comfort* one another with these *words*" (1 Thess. 4:18).

The Puritans called this "conference"—the practice of intentional godly conversation with fellow believers.[16] Richard Rogers includes it among his list of means for pursuing godliness in *Seven Treatises*, and in *The Great Gain of Godliness*, Thomas Watson shows what godly conversation entails:

> *Christians, when they meet together, should use holy conference....* Have not you matter enough in the Word to furnish you with something to say? Let me suggest a few

---

15. Owen, "Mutual Care," in *Works*, 16:479–80.

16. See Joanne J. Jung, *Godly Conversations: Rediscovering the Puritan Practice of Conference* (Grand Rapids: Reformation Heritage Books, 2011).

things to you. When you meet, speak one to another of the *promises*. No honey is so sweet, as that which drops from a promise! The promises are the support of faith, the springs of joy, and the saints' royal charter. Are you citizens of heaven, and yet do not speak of your royal charter?

Speak of the *preciousness of Christ*. He is all beauty and love; he has laid down his blood as the price of your redemption. Have you a friend who has redeemed you, and yet you never speak of him?

Speak one to another of *sin*, what a deadly evil it is....

Speak of the beauty of *holiness*, which is the soul's embroidery, filling it with such...splendor, as makes God and angels fall in love with it....

Speak one to another of your *souls*: enquire whether they are in health.

Speak about *death* and *eternity*: can you belong to heaven and not speak of your country?[17]

We also see many examples of this practice in *Pilgrim's Progress* in Christian's conversations with Interpreter and with the porter and damsels in Palace Beautiful, not to mention his traveling companions. For example, when Christian and Hopeful battle slumber on Enchanted Ground, they do so by means of talking about spiritual matters. "To prevent drowsiness in this place, let us fall into good discourse," Christian says to Hopeful.[18] Just so. Godly conversation with other believers is one of the most important strategies for keeping a wakeful, watching heart.

---

17. Thomas Watson, *The Great Gain of Godliness* (Edinburgh: Banner of Truth Trust, 2006), 62, 69–70.

18. Bunyan, *Pilgrim's Progress*, 158.

Admonition

A second way to practice mutual watchfulness is by admonition. Paul writes, "Now I myself am confident concerning you, my brethren, that you also are full of goodness, filled with all knowledge, able also to admonish one another" (Rom. 15:14). The Greek word "admonish" is *noutheteō*. According to one lexicon, this word means "to counsel about avoidance or cessation of an improper course of conduct."[19] It means not only to instruct but to warn.

Owen also connects admonition to watchfulness in his *Rules for Walking in Fellowship*, a brief book that outlines the biblical duties church members have toward their pastors and toward one another. Here is one of Owen's rules: "Watch vigilantly over each other's lives, mutually admonish in cases of disorderly walking, and render an account to the church if the offending party will not be prevailed upon."[20]

Owen says that "a threefold duty is included here: watchfulness, admonition (the primary focus of this rule), and, where necessary, discipline."[21] But while this duty certainly includes the more formal aspects of church discipline, it also involves the less formal (though no less important) aspects of brotherly love expressed in mutual admonition.

In discussing the fraternal, brother-to-brother dimension of this responsibility, Owen asserts "that it is the duty of every church member toward those with whom he walks

---

19. Ardnt, Danker, and Bauer, *Greek-English Lexicon*, 679.

20. John Owen, *Rules for Walking in Fellowship* (Grand Rapids: Reformation Heritage Books, 2014), 81. This is a modernized version of Owen's book edited by David G. Whitla. For the original, see Owen, *Eshcol: A Cluster of the Fruit of Canaan*, in *Works*, 13:83.

21. Owen, *Rules for Walking*, 83. See also *Eshcol*, in *Works*, 13:84.

Eight Directions for
Admonishing Others

In *Rules for Walking in Fellowship*, John Owen reminds believers of the need for "much caution and wisdom, tenderness and moderation" in admonishing others and includes eight things for believers to consider when called upon to admonish others.

1. That in the whole action he does not transgress the rule of charity which we find in 1 Corinthians 13:7 and Galatians 6:1–5.

2. Let him have peace at home by constantly laboring to cast out all beams and specks from his own eye (Matt. 7:5).

3. Let him so perform it that it may evidently appear that he has no other aim but the glory of God and the good of his reproved brother—all envy and rejoicing in evil being far away.

4. Let him be sure to draw his admonitions from the Word, that the authority of God may appear in them, and without the Word let him not presume to speak.

5. Let all the external circumstances of the admonition, such as the time, place, persons, and the like, be carefully weighed, so that all provocations in the least manner may be fully avoided.

6. Let it be considered as an ordinance that Christ has a special regard for.

7. Let him carefully distinguish between personal injuries to himself—whose mention calls more for forgiveness than reproof—and other offenses tending to public scandal.

8. Lastly, let self-examination for the same or similar failings always accompany our brotherly admonition.[a]

---

a. John Owen, *Rules for Walking in Fellowship* (Grand Rapids: Reformation Heritage Books, 2014), 84–85; see also Owen, *Eshcol: A Cluster of the Fruit of Canaan*, in *Works*, 13:84–85.

in fellowship to admonish from the Word any whom he sees walking with unsound footing, as becomes the gospel, and by this means to recover his soul to the right way."[22]

Consideration

The third means of practicing mutual watchfulness is consideration. I draw this word from Hebrews 10:24–25: "And let us consider one another in order to stir up love and good works, not forsaking the assembling of ourselves together, as is the manner of some, but exhorting one another, and so much the more as you see the Day approaching." Notice that the direct object of the verb "consider"—who we are to consider—is "one another." And the purpose of considering one another is "to stir up love and good works." This is a call to study our fellow believers with the aim of helping them grow. In such relationships, spiritual friendship becomes a means of mutual watchfulness and spiritual growth.

Such friendships were characteristic of M'Cheyne, whom I've quoted so often in this book. Andrew Bonar describes M'Cheyne's friendship with Alexander Somerville in terms of mutual watching:

Somerville...was his familiar friend and companion in...his youth. And he, too, about this time, having been brought to taste the powers of the world to come, they united their efforts for each other's welfare. They met together for the study of the Bible, and used to exercise themselves in the Septuagint Greek and the Hebrew original. But oftener still they met for prayer and solemn converse; and, carrying on all their studies

---

22. Owen, *Rules*, 84. See also *Eshcol*, in *Works*, 13:84.

in the same spirit, watched each other's steps in the narrow way.[23]

"They united their efforts for each other's welfare" and "watched each other's steps in the narrow way." This is what it means to "consider one another in order to stir up love and good works." This is the key to mutual watchfulness and the irreducible core to true Christian friendship.

Watchfulness and the Church

The main point of this chapter is that you need the church. Watchfulness is not like playing solitaire. Though watching is a discipline, it is not a solo sport.

We cannot effectively watch ourselves without others. We need pastors who watch for our souls. We need brothers and sisters to exhort and admonish us to keep our eyes on Jesus, to stir us from spiritual drowsiness through godly conversation. We need companions on our pilgrimage to heaven. We need spiritual friendship.

Examine and Apply

1. Watchfulness is a community project. Do you agree with this statement? Why or why not?

2. Scripture uses several metaphors for spiritual leadership. What are these metaphors, and what do they suggest about the roles of pastors and elders in the local church?

23. Bonar, *Memoir & Remains*, 12.

3. If you are a pastor, prayerfully read through appendix 2, "The Minister's Self-Watch." Ask the Lord to help you honestly assess your life and ministry. If you're not a minister, stop now to pray for your pastor.

4. Have you ever been on the receiving end of restoration, as described in Galatians 6:1–2? Think through your experience. What happened, and how did the Lord use it to bring you back to Him?

5. Read through Owen's directions for admonishing others. How would following these directions improve your relationships with fellow believers?

6. Who helps you watch? If spiritual friendships are missing from your life, ask the Lord to bring you such a friend. Consider sharing this book with someone in your church or fellowship group and meeting regularly to discuss the questions for each chapter.

Conclusion

You have now reached the end of this book, but not of your watch. Your race is unfinished, your journey incomplete. Your warfare rages on. Until Christ returns or takes you home, you still have battles to fight. Only when your body is laid to rest and your soul awakes in glory will your watch be over.

I've referred often in this book to *The Holy War*, Bunyan's allegorical saga of how Christ conquers Satan and recaptures the human heart. In the final chapter, Emmanuel gathers the townspeople on an appointed day to give them a compelling, rousing speech. He first reminds Mansoul that she is the beloved of his heart, whom he has chosen, redeemed, and reconciled to himself. The gracious prince then recounts how he defeated Diabolus and recovered Mansoul for his father and how he not only installed many captains and soldiers within the city but also set Mr. Godly-fear to work within her and healed her from her backslidings.

Emmanuel next points to Mansoul's glorious future, when he will relocate the city to his father's kingdom, there to be a spectacle of wonder, a monument of mercy, and the holy habitation of God. This, after all, was the purpose for which Mansoul was first built. In that day, they will be rid of the

wicked Diabolonians once and for all. There in the royal city,
Emmanuel promises, they will join the rest of the redeemed to
enjoy the treasures laid up for them by his father.

The king's son then shows Mansoul her present duty.
She is to keep her garments white, washing them often in the
fountain he has provided for their cleansing. She must also
bear his love in mind, remembering that he lived and died for
them and that because he lives, they will live also. Emmanuel
warns that nothing can hurt them nor grieve him nor make
them fall before their enemies—except sin. Therefore, they
are to take heed of sin, to stand against their enemies, and
to prize Emmanuel's noble captains and his mercy.[1] At the
climax of this charge, Emmanuel entreats Mansoul with these
urgent, moving words:

> Remember, therefore, O my Mansoul, that thou art
> beloved of me; as I have therefore taught thee to watch,
> to fight, to pray, and to make war against my foes, so now
> I command thee to believe that my love is constant to
> thee. O my Mansoul, how have I set my heart, my love
> upon thee! Watch! Behold, I lay none other burden upon
> thee than what thou hast already. Hold fast till I come![2]

This is the watchfulness we need. Assailed and assaulted
by our foes we may be. But we are Christ's dearly loved people. He has commanded us to watch, fight, and pray, all the
while trusting and cherishing His unwavering love. Watch
your life and keep your heart, dear Christian. But for every
look at yourself, take ten looks at Christ, the one who lived,
died, and rose for you.

---

1. Bunyan, *Holy War*, 280–86.
2. Bunyan, *Holy War*, 286.

Appendix 1
M'Cheyne's Personal Reformation

About this time he wrote down, for his own use, an examination into things that ought to be amended and changed. I subjoin it entire. How singularly close and impartial are these researches into his soul! How acute is he in discovering his variations from the holy law of God! Oh that we all were taught by the same spirit thus to try our reins! It is only when we are thus thoroughly experiencing our helplessness, and discovering the thousand forms of indwelling sin, that we really sit as disciples at Christ's feet, and gladly receive Him as all in all! And at each such moment we feel in the Spirit of Ignatius, "It is only now that I begin to be a disciple."

Mr. M'Cheyne entitles the examination of his heart and life "Reformation," and it commences thus:

It is the duty of ministers in this day to begin the reformation of religion and manners with themselves, families, etc., with confession of past sin, earnest prayer for direction, grace, and full purpose of heart. Malachi 3:3—"He shall purify the sons of Levi." Ministers are probably laid aside for a time for this very purpose.

Excerpted from Bonar, *Memoir & Remains*, 149–58.

Personal Reformation

I am persuaded that I shall obtain the highest amount of present happiness, I shall do most for God's glory and the good of man, and I shall have the fullest reward in eternity, by maintaining a conscience always washed in Christ's blood, by being filled with the Holy Spirit at all times, and by attaining the most entire likeness to Christ in mind, will, and heart, that is possible for a redeemed sinner to attain to in this world.

I am persuaded that whenever any one from without, or my own heart from within, at any moment, or in any circumstances, contradicts this—if any one shall insinuate that it is not for my present and eternal happiness, and for God's glory and my usefulness, to maintain a blood-washed conscience, to be entirely filled with the Spirit, and to be fully conformed to the image of Christ in all things—that is the voice of the devil, God's enemy, the enemy of my soul and of all good— the most foolish, wicked, and miserable of all the creatures. See Proverbs 9:17—"Stolen waters are sweet."

1. To maintain a conscience void of offence, I am persuaded that I ought to confess my sins more. I think I ought to confess sin the moment I see it to be sin; whether I am in company, or in study, or even preaching, the soul ought to cast a glance of abhorrence at the sin. If I go on with the duty, leaving the sin unconfessed, I go on with a burdened conscience, and add sin to sin. I think I ought at certain times of the day—my best times—say, after breakfast and after tea—to confess solemnly the sins of the previous hours, and to seek their complete remission.

I find that the devil often makes use of the confession of sin to stir up again the very sin confessed into new exercise, so that I am afraid to dwell upon the confession. I must ask experienced Christians about this. For the present, I think I should strive against this awful abuse of confession, whereby the devil seeks to frighten me away from confessing. I ought to take all methods for seeing the vileness of my sins. I ought to regard myself as a condemned branch of Adam—as partaker of a nature opposite to God from the womb (Ps. 51)—as having a heart full of all wickedness, which pollutes every thought, word, and action, during my whole life, from birth to death. I ought to confess often the sins of my youth, like David and Paul—my sins before conversion, my sins since conversion—sins against light and knowledge, against love and grace, against each person of the Godhead. I ought to look at my sins in the light of the holy law, in the light of God's countenance, in the light of the cross, in the light of the judgment-seat, in the light of hell, in the light of eternity. I ought to examine my dreams—my floating thoughts—my predilections—my often recurring actions—my habits of thought, feeling, speech, and action—the slanders of my enemies, and the reproofs, and even banterings, of my friends—to find out traces of my prevailing sin, matter for confession. I ought to have a stated day of confession, with fasting—say, once a month. I ought to have a number of scriptures marked, to bring sin to remembrance. I ought to make use of all bodily affliction, domestic trial, frowns of providence on myself, house, parish, church, or country, as calls from God to confess sin. The sins and afflictions of other men should call me to the same. I ought, on Sabbath evenings, and on Communion Sabbath evenings, to be especially careful to confess the sins of holy things. I ought to confess the sins of my confessions— their imperfections, sinful aims, self-righteous tendency,

etc.—and to look to Christ as having confessed my sins per-
fectly over his own sacrifice.

I ought to go to Christ for the forgiveness of each sin.
In washing my body, I go over every spot, and wash it out.
Should I be less careful in washing my soul? I ought to see
the stripe that was made on the back of Jesus by each of my
sins. I ought to see the infinite pang thrill through the soul of
Jesus equal to an eternity of my hell for my sins, and for all of
them. I ought to see that in Christ's bloodshedding there is an
infinite over-payment for all my sins. Although Christ did not
suffer more than infinite justice demanded, yet He could not
suffer at all without laying down an infinite ransom.

I feel, when I have sinned, an immediate reluctance to go
to Christ. I am ashamed to go. I feel as if it would do no good
to go—as if it were making Christ a minister of sin, to go
straight from the swine-trough to the best robe—and a thousand other excuses; but I am persuaded they are all lies, direct
from hell. John argues the opposite way: "If any man sin, we
have an advocate with the Father"; Jeremiah 3:1 and a thousand other scriptures are against it. I am sure there is neither
peace nor safety from deeper sin, but in going directly to the
Lord Jesus Christ. This is God's way of peace and holiness. It
is folly to the world and the beclouded heart, but it is the way.

I must never think a sin too small to need immediate application to the blood of Christ. If I put away a good
conscience, concerning faith I make shipwreck. I must never
think my sins too great, too aggravated, too presumptuous—
as when done on my knees, or in preaching, or by a dying
bed, or during dangerous illness—to hinder me from fleeing
to Christ. The weight of my sins should act like the weight of
a clock: the heavier it is, it makes it go the faster.

I must not only wash in Christ's blood, but clothe me in Christ's obedience. For every sin of omission in self, I may find a divinely perfect obedience ready for me in Christ. For every sin of commission in self, I may find not only a stripe or a wound in Christ, but also a perfect rendering of the opposite obedience in my place, so that the law is magnified, its curse more than carried, its demand more than answered.

Often the doctrine of Christ for me appears common, well known, having nothing new in it; and I am tempted to pass it by and go to some scripture more taking. This is the devil again—a red-hot lie. Christ for us is ever new, ever glorious. "Unsearchable riches of Christ"—an infinite object, and the only one for a guilty soul. I ought to have a number of scriptures ready, which lead my blind soul directly to Christ, such as Isaiah 45, Romans 3.

2. To be filled with the Holy Spirit, I am persuaded that I ought to study more my own weakness. I ought to have a number of scriptures ready to be meditated on, such as Romans 7, John 15, to convince me that I am a helpless worm.

I am tempted to think that I am now an established Christian—that I have overcome this or that lust so long—that I have got into the habit of the opposite grace,—so that there is no fear; I may venture very near the temptation—nearer than other men. This is a lie of Satan. I might as well speak of gunpowder getting by habit a power of resisting fire, so as not to catch the spark. As long as powder is wet, it resists the spark; but when it becomes dry, it is ready to explode at the first touch. As long as the Spirit dwells in my heart He deadens me to sin, so that, if lawfully called through temptation, I may reckon upon God carrying me through. But when the Spirit leaves me, I am like dry gunpowder. Oh for a sense of this!

I am tempted to think that there are some sins for which I have no natural taste, such as strong drink, profane language, etc., so that I need not fear temptation to such sins. This is a lie—a proud, presumptuous lie. The seeds of all sins are in my heart, and perhaps all the more dangerously that I do not see them.

I ought to pray and labor for the deepest sense of my utter weakness and helplessness that ever a sinner was brought to feel. I am helpless in respect of every lust that ever was, or ever will be, in the human heart. I am a worm—a beast—before God. I often tremble to think that this is true. I feel as if it would not be safe for me to renounce all indwelling strength, as if it would be dangerous for me to feel (what is the truth) that there is nothing in me keeping me back from the grossest and vilest sin. This is a delusion of the devil. My only safety is to know, feel, and confess my helplessness, that I may hang upon the arm of Omnipotence…. I daily wish that sin had been rooted out of my heart. I say, "Why did God leave the root of lasciviousness, pride, anger, etc., in my bosom? He hates sin, and I hate it; why did He not take it clean away?" I know many answers to this which completely satisfy my judgment, but still I do not feel satisfied. This is wrong. It is right to be weary of the being of sin, but not right to quarrel with my present "good fight of faith."… The falls of professors into sin make me tremble. I have been driven away from prayer, and burdened in a fearful manner by hearing or seeing their sin. This is wrong. It is right to tremble, and to make every sin of every professor a lesson of my own helplessness; but it should lead me the more to Christ…. If I were more deeply convinced of my utter helplessness, I think I would not be so alarmed when I hear of the falls of other men.... I should study those sins in which I am most helpless, in which passion becomes like a whirlwind and I like a straw. No figure of speech can represent my utter want of power to resist the torrent of sin.... I ought to study Christ's omnipotence more: Hebrews 7:25, 1 Thessalonians 5:23, Romans 6:14, Romans 5:9, 10, and such scriptures, should be ever before me.... Paul's thorn, 2 Corinthians 12, is the experience of the greater part of my life. It should be ever before me.... There are many subsidiary methods of seeking deliverance from sins, which must not be neglected—thus, marriage (1 Cor. 7:2); fleeing (1 Tim. 6:11; 1 Cor. 6:18); watch and pray (Matt. 26:41); the word, "It is written, It is written." So Christ defended himself; Matthew 4.... But the main defense is casting myself into the arms of Christ like a helpless child, and beseeching Him to fill me with the Holy Spirit. "This is the victory that overcometh the world, even our faith"—1 John 5:4, 5, a wonderful passage.

I ought to study Christ as a living Savior more—as a Shepherd, carrying the sheep He finds—as a King, reigning in and over the souls He has redeemed—as a Captain, fighting with those who fight with me (Psalm 35)—as one who has engaged to bring me through all temptations and trials, however impossible to flesh and blood.

I am often tempted to say, "How can this Man save us? How can Christ in heaven deliver me from lusts which I feel raging in me, and nets I feel enclosing me?" This is the father of lies again! "He is able to save unto the uttermost."

I ought to study Christ as an Intercessor. He prayed most for Peter, who was to be most tempted. I am on his breast-plate. If I could hear Christ praying for me in the next room,

I would not fear a million of enemies. Yet the distance makes no difference; He is praying for me.

I ought to study the Comforter more—his Godhead, his love, his almightiness. I have found by experience that nothing sanctifies me so much as meditating on the Comforter, as John 14:16. And yet how seldom I do this! Satan keeps me from it. I am often like those men who said, They knew not if there be any Holy Ghost.... I ought never to forget that my body is dwelt in by the third Person of the Godhead. The very thought of this should make me tremble to sin; 1 Corinthians 6.... I ought never to forget that sin grieves the Holy Spirit—vexes and quenches Him.... If I would be filled with the Spirit, I feel I must read the Bible more, pray more, and watch more.

3. To gain entire likeness to Christ, I ought to get a high esteem of the happiness of it. I am persuaded that God's happiness is inseparably linked in with his holiness. Holiness and happiness are like light and heat. God never tasted one of the pleasures of sin.

Christ had a body such as I have, yet He never tasted one of the pleasures of sin. The redeemed, through all eternity, will never taste one of the pleasures of sin; yet their happiness is complete. It would be my greatest happiness to be from this moment entirely like them. Every sin is something away from my greatest enjoyment.... The devil strives night and day to make me forget this or disbelieve it. He says, "Why should you not enjoy this pleasure as much as Solomon or David? You may go to heaven also." I am persuaded that this is a lie—that my true happiness is to go and sin no more.

I ought not to delay parting with sins. Now is God's time. "I made haste and delayed not."... I ought not to spare sins because I have long allowed them as infirmities, and others would think it odd if I were to change all at once. What a wretched delusion of Satan that is!

Whatever I see to be sin, I ought from this hour to set my whole soul against it, using all scriptural methods to mortify it—as the Scriptures, special prayer for the Spirit, fasting, watching.

I ought to mark strictly the occasions when I have fallen, and avoid the occasion as much as the sin itself.

Satan often tempts me to go as near to temptations as possible without committing the sin. This is fearful—tempting God and grieving the Holy Ghost. It is a deep-laid plot of Satan.

I ought to flee all temptation, according to Proverbs 4:15—Avoid it, pass not by it, turn from it, and pass away.... I ought constantly to pour out my heart to God, praying for entire conformity to Christ—for the whole law to be written on my heart.... I ought statedly and solemnly to give my heart to God—to surrender my all into His everlasting arms, according to the prayer, Psalm 31, "Into thine hand I commit my spirit"—beseeching Him not to let any iniquity, secret or presumptuous, have dominion over me, and to fill me with every grace that is in Christ, in the highest degree that it is possible for a redeemed sinner to receive it, and at all times, till death.

I ought to meditate often on heaven as a world of holiness—where all are holy, where the joy is holy joy, the work holy work; so that, without personal holiness, I never can be there.... I ought to avoid the appearance of evil. God commands me; and I find that Satan has a singular art in linking the appearance and reality together.

I find that speaking of some sins defiles my mind and leads me into temptation; and I find that God forbids even saints to speak of the things that are done of them in secret. I ought to avoid this.

Eve, Achan, David, all fell through the lust of the eye. I should make a covenant with mine, and pray, "Turn away mine eyes from viewing vanity.".... Satan makes unconverted men like the deaf adder to the sound of the gospel. I should pray to be made deaf by the Holy Spirit to all that would tempt me to sin.

One of my most frequent occasions of being led into temptation is this—I say it is needful to my office that I listen to this, or look into this, or speak of this. So far this is true; yet I am sure Satan has his part in this argument. I should seek divine direction to settle how far it will be good for my ministry, and how far evil for my soul, that I may avoid the latter.

I am persuaded that nothing is thriving in my soul unless it is growing. "Grow in grace." "Lord, increase our faith." "Forgetting the things that are behind.".... I am persuaded that I ought to be inquiring at God and man what grace I want, and how I may become more like Christ.... I ought to strive for more purity, humility, meekness, patience under suffering, love. "Make me Christ-like in all things," should be my constant prayer. "Fill me with the Holy Spirit."

Reformation in Secret Prayer

I ought not to omit any of the parts of prayer—confession, adoration, thanksgiving, petition, and intercession.

There is a fearful tendency to omit confession, proceeding from low views of God and His law, slight views of my heart and the sins of my past life. This must be resisted. There is a constant tendency to omit adoration, when I forget to whom I am speaking—when I rush heedlessly into the presence of Jehovah, without remembering His awful name and character—when I have little eyesight for His glory, and little admiration of His wonders. "Where are the wise?" I have the native tendency of the heart to omit giving thanks. And yet it is specially commanded (Phil. 4:6). Often when the heart is selfish, dead to the salvation of others, I omit intercession. And yet it especially is the spirit of the great Advocate, who has the name of Israel always on his heart.

Perhaps every prayer need not have all these: but surely a day should not pass without some space being devoted to each.

I ought to pray before seeing any one. Often when I sleep long, or meet with others early, and then have family prayer, and breakfast, and forenoon callers, often it is eleven or twelve o'clock before I begin secret prayer. This is a wretched system. It is unscriptural. Christ rose before day, and went into a solitary place. David says, "Early will I seek Thee; Thou shalt early hear my voice." Mary Magdalene came to the sepulchre while it was yet dark. Family prayer loses much of its power and sweetness; and I can do no good to those who come to seek from me. The conscience feels guilty, the soul unfed, the lamp not trimmed. Then, when secret prayer comes, the soul is often out of tune. I feel it is far better to begin with God— to see His face first—to get my soul near Him before it is near another. "When I awake I am still with Thee."

If I have slept too long, or am going an early journey, or my time is any way shortened, it is best to dress hurriedly, and have a few minutes alone with God, than to give it up for lost.

But, in general, it is best to have at least one hour alone with God, before engaging in anything else. At the same time, I must be careful not to reckon communion with God by minutes or hours, or by solitude. I have pored over my Bible, and on my knees for hours, with little or no communion; and my times of solitude have been often times of greatest temptation.

As to intercession, I ought daily to intercede for my own family, connections, relatives, and friends; also for my flock—the believers, the awakened, the careless; the sick, the bereaved; the poor, the rich; my elders, Sabbath-school teachers, day-school teachers, children, tract-distributors—that all means may be blessed: Sabbath-day preaching and teaching; visiting of the sick, visiting from house to house; providences, sacraments. I ought daily to intercede briefly for the whole town, the Church of Scotland, all faithful ministers; for vacant congregations, students of divinity, etc.; for dear brethren by name; for missionaries to Jews and Gentiles—and for this end I must read missionary intelligence regularly, and get acquainted with all that is doing throughout the world. It would stir me up to pray with the map before me. I must have a scheme of prayer also the names of missionaries marked on the map. I ought to intercede at large for the above on Saturday morning and evening from seven to eight. Perhaps also I might take different parts for different days; only I ought daily to plead for my family and flock. I ought to pray in everything. "Be careful for nothing, but in everything…by prayer and supplication, make your requests known unto God." Often I receive a letter asking me to preach, or some such request.

I find myself answering before having asked counsel of God. Still oftener a person calls and asks me something, and I do not ask direction. Often I go out to visit a sick person in a hurry, without asking His blessing, which alone can make the visit of any use. I am persuaded that I ought never to do anything without prayer, and, if possible, special, secret prayer.

In reading the history of the Church of Scotland, I see how much her troubles and trials have been connected with the salvation of souls and the glory of Christ. I ought to pray far more for our church, for our leading ministers by name, and for my own clear guidance in the right way, that I may not be led aside, or driven aside, from following Christ. Many difficult questions may be forced on us for which I am not fully prepared, such as the lawfulness of covenants. I should pray much more in peaceful days, that I may be guided rightly when days of trial come.

I ought to spend the best hours of the day in communion with God. It is my noblest and most fruitful employment, and is not to be thrust into any corner. The morning hours, from six to eight, are the most uninterrupted, and should be thus employed, if I can prevent drowsiness. A little time after breakfast might be given to intercession. After tea is my best hour, and that should be solemnly dedicated to God, if possible.

I ought not to give up the good old habit of prayer before going to bed; but guard must be kept against sleep. Planning what things I am to ask is the best remedy. When I awake in the night, I ought to rise and pray, as David and as John Welsh did.

I ought to read three chapters of the Bible in secret every day, at least.

I ought on Sabbath morning to look over all the chapters read through the week, and especially the verses marked. I ought to read in three different places; I ought also to read according to subjects, lives, etc.

He has evidently left this unfinished, and now he knows even as he is known.

Appendix 2
The Minister's Self-Watch

When Paul charged the Ephesian elders to watch over the flock, he also exhorted them to watch over themselves. "Therefore take heed to *yourselves* and to all the flock, among which the Holy Spirit has made you overseers, to shepherd the church of God which He purchased with His own blood" (Acts 20:28). And in his letters to young Timothy, Paul said, "Take heed to *yourself* and to the doctrine. Continue in them, for in doing this you will save both yourself and those who hear you.... *Be watchful in all things*, endure afflictions, do the work of an evangelist, fulfill your ministry" (1 Tim. 4:16; 2 Tim. 4:5).

In his *Lectures to My Students*, Charles Spurgeon called this "The Minister's Self-Watch." Beginning with the common observation that every workman must keep his tools in good repair, Spurgeon reminds us that "we are, in a certain sense, our own tools, and therefore must keep ourselves in order."[1]

If the axe is not regularly sharpened, its edge will quickly dull. If a musician fails to tune her instrument, she will

---

1. C. H. Spurgeon, *Lectures to My Students* (Pasadena, Tex.: Pilgrim Publications, 1990), 1.

produce discord, not harmony. So with us: if we do not keep our moral sensibilities sharp and our hearts attuned to God, we will lose our cutting edge in ministry and produce dissonant noise that hinders our ministries.

No one has said this more eloquently than M'Cheyne in his 1840 letter to Dan Edwards:

> Do not forget the culture of the inner man,—I mean of the heart. How diligently the cavalry officer keeps his sabre clean and sharp; every stain he rubs off with the greatest care. Remember you are God's sword,—his instrument,—I trust a chosen vessel unto Him to bear his name. In great measure, according to the purity and perfections of the instrument, will be the success. It is not great talents God blesses so much as great likeness to Jesus. A holy minister is an awful weapon in the hand of God.[2]

Spurgeon also quoted M'Cheyne and, in the rest of his lecture, outlined just what this kind of watchfulness entails.

First, ministers must be sure *they are saved men.*[3] "How horrible," Spurgeon writes, "to be a preacher of the gospel and yet to be un-converted!"[4] Spurgeon quotes Richard Baxter's solemn warning to pastors:

> Take heed to yourselves lest you should be void of that saving grace of God which you offer to others, and be strangers to the effectual working of that gospel which you preach; and lest, while you proclaim the necessity of a Savior to the world, your hearts should neglect him,

---

2. Robert Murray M'Cheyne to Dan Edwards, October 2, 1840, in Bonar, *Memoir & Remains*, 282.

3. Spurgeon, *Lectures to My Students*, 3.

4. Spurgeon, *Lectures to My Students*, 4.

and you should miss of an interest in him and his saving benefits. Take heed to yourselves, lest you perish while you call upon others to take heed of perishing; and lest you famish yourselves while you prepare food for them.[5]

Second, pastors should also be sure *their piety is vigorous*.[6] The pastor must be a mature believer, not a novice in the faith. "His pulse of vital godliness must beat strongly and regularly; his eye of faith must be bright; his foot of resolution must be firm; his hand of activity must be quick; his whole inner man must be in the highest degree of sanity."[7] As Paul told Timothy, so every minister should seek to be "an example to the believers in word, in conduct, in love, in spirit, in faith, in purity" (1 Tim. 4:12).

In another of his letters, M'Cheyne similarly advised W. C. Burns, reminding him of the means for maintaining a healthy soul. "Take heed to *thyself*," he said. "Your own soul is your first and greatest care. You know a sound body alone can work with power; much more a *healthy soul*. Keep a clear conscience through the blood of the Lamb. Keep up close communion with God. Study likeness to Him in all things. Read the Bible for your own growth first, then for your people."[8] The key to soul health, then, is a blood-washed conscience, intimate fellowship with God, conformity to Christ, and devotion to the Scriptures. This means that no amount

5. Richard Baxter, *The Reformed Pastor* (Edinburgh: Banner of Truth, 1999), 53, as quoted in Spurgeon, *Lectures to My Students*, 6–7.

6. Spurgeon, *Lectures to My Students*, 7.

7. Spurgeon, *Lectures to My Students*, 8.

8. Robert Murray M'Cheyne to Rev. W. C. Burns, March 22, 1839, in Bonar, *Memoir & Remains*, 216–17.

of theological training, communication acumen, or leadership skills can substitute for personal piety.

John Owen also emphasizes this, reminding pastors of their need for an "experience of the power of the truth which they preach in and upon their own souls."[9] In other words, it isn't enough to know the truth. We must also experience its saving, sanctifying influence—its power—in our hearts.

M'Cheyne was himself a great example of this. His friend and biographer, Andrew Bonar, said that he "fed others by what he himself was feeding upon. His preaching was in a manner the development of his soul's experience."[10] And that's exactly what Owen was after: "A man preacheth that sermon only well unto others which preacheth itself in his own soul. And he that doth not feed on and thrive in the digestion of the food which he provides for others will scarce make it savoury unto them.... If the word do not dwell with power in us, it will not pass with power from us."[11]

Third, Spurgeon says the minister's *personal character should agree in all respects with his ministry.*[12] To put it most simply: his life must match his doctrine, and his walk must be congruent with his talk. This is not a requirement for sinless perfection, as if that were even possible. What it does require is a heart well exercised in the graces of faith and repentance. It demands the ongoing pursuit of holiness and the regular mortification of sin. And it entails the maintenance of a blameless life that both honors Christ and safeguards His church.

9. Owen, *The True Nature of a Gospel Church and Its Government*, in *Works*, 16:76.

10. Bonar, *Memoir & Remains*, 36.

11. Owen, *True Nature of a Gospel Church*, in *Works*, 16:76.

12. Spurgeon, *Lectures to My Students*, 12.

Nothing could be more relevant to the contemporary church. We have seen far too many pastors fall into scandalous sin. We have all heard the reports of celebrity preachers now infamous for their moral failures. And we all know the devastating stories of men once mighty with God who are now casualties of war. When I hear these reports, I tremble. I pray. And I seek to renew my watch. No Christian, and certainly no pastor, is invulnerable to temptation.

The truth is we are weak and frail and left to ourselves will fall. Let all of us, then, and not least of all pastors, cast ourselves on the Lord at this moment. And let us keep ourselves in the love of God (Jude 21), even as we trust the One

> who is able to keep [us] from stumbling,
> And to present [us] faultless
> Before the presence of His glory with exceeding joy,

to whom

> Be glory and majesty,
> Dominion and power,
> Both now and forever.
> Amen. (Jude 24–25)